With

[signature]

November 23, 2006

Discovering Music from the Inside Out
An Autobiography

Discovering Music from the Inside Out

An Autobiography

Edwin Elias Gordon

GIA Publications, Inc.
Chicago

G-6762
© 2006 GIA Publications, Inc.
7404 S. Mason Ave., Chicago, IL 60638
www.giamusic.com
ISBN: 1-57999-569-1

Cover design and layout: Robert M. Sacha

All rights reserved.
Printed in the United States of America

To Carol, Jaime, Pamela, and Carrie

Contents

Preface ix

I The Early Years (1927-1945) 1
   Stamford, Connecticut, Family, String Bass,
   Sid Wiess, Milton Kestenbaum

II Glimpse of the Future (1945-1956) 13
    U.S. Army, Eastman School of Music, Marriage,
    New York, Gene Krupa, Eastman Revisited,
    Philip Sklar, Ohio University, Neal Glenn

III Delight and Disillusion (1956-1972) 45
     University of Iowa, Al Hieronymous, Early
     Publications, Musical Aptitude Profile, Learning and
     Teaching, Research Studies, Divorce

IV Pausing and Passing Midway
    (1972-1979) 73
    State University of New York at Buffalo,
    (SUNYAB), Marriage, GIA, Snow, More Research
    and Tests, Tonal and Rhythm Patterns,
    Developmental Music Aptitude, Rhythm
    and Rhythm Solfege, Audiation

V The Philadelphia Story (1979-1997) 93
   Temple University, PhD Program, Faculty,
   Sugarloaf Seminars, Gordon Institute
   for Music Learning (GIML), Overseas Lectures,
   Exposure

VI Philosophy, Art, and Retirement
    (1979-1997, continued) 111
    Incorporating Learning into Teaching,
    Early Childhood Music, Improvisation,
    More About Research, MENC,
    Goodbye to the Bass, Sculpturing

VII More to Come (1997-present) 133
    University of South Carolina, Archive,
    Harmonic Patterns and Research,
    Michigan State University,
    European and Asian GIML Chapters,
    More Publications, More Art

    Publications 143

Preface

For the vast majority of persons who courageously choose to write an autobiography, the act is a once-in-a-lifetime endeavor. It has been with considerable trepidation I have undertaken the task, but having been so driven through my adult life to examine the music learning process, I am often asked what in my personal life could have inspired and directed me to probe this facet of what was to become understood, in the full sense of the word, as audiation.

Although I know of no specific answer, I must confess each research project generates enormous excitement and poses more questions to be pursued. The fervor then builds as research results are evaluated and disseminated. Books and articles must be written to share the findings and to explain how they may be put to practical use in helping children and students of all ages develop their understanding of music. I have had no choice.

As I state in the book, there have been some outstanding persons who entered my life at exactly the time their astuteness was most essential in helping me grow both professionally and personally—fine and caring bass teachers; academic mentors; publishers; professional musicians; my wife, Carol; and even colleagues and leaders of professional organizations with whom I have strong ideological disagreements.

In essence, this is much more a professional autobiography than a personal one. Those who know me are aware that my professional life began to overtake my personal life from the time I became entranced by music as a bass player. There are no diaries and very few letters contain information that might have been included in a book such as this, so I had to reveal as much as possible simply from memory. I have described what I consider to be relevant and of interest and take full responsibility for errors of omission and commission. It is my hope that this book will supplement and support (or contradict, if necessary) reports of later biographers, and I disavow any vindictive or malicious intent. My apologies to anyone I may have unintentionally ignored, misrepresented, or misjudged.

In keeping with a self-imposed disposition, I make every effort to be thorough, but I work fast to accomplish what I believe to be necessary. Never could I have presented the hundreds of lectures, written the number of books, tests, and articles, or completed the amount of research that I have had I not been motivated in this way. Nonetheless, many years ago, one of my beloved bass teachers, Philip Sklar, said to me, "Don't be in such a hurry." I'm afraid I never took his advice.

Edwin E. Gordon
Columbia, South Carolina
2005

I
The Early Years
(1927–1945)

A column in the October 12, 1927, edition of the *Stamford Advocate* was titled "Sixty-Three Children Born Here during August and September." Among those listed was

> Elias, son of Mr. and Mrs.
> Martin Gordon, at Stamford
> Hospital, September 14.

• • •

Unfortunately, my birth certificate read Edwin Elias Gordon, even though throughout my adult life I would have preferred the name Elias. My family always used the name Edwin. A change would have caused considerable confusion after my professional life had been established, so I have reluctantly allowed the years to pass with my being called Edwin, but I have always insisted that the "E" for Elias be present in all publication and business endeavors.

Many elements of my early life seem almost enigmatic. I remember only patches of isolated incidents as I am subjected to occasional flashbacks (primarily unpleasant ones) from my childhood. My father's business was the Stamford Awning Works, which made and installed awnings, Venetian blinds, and shades and constructed tents and canopies for special business and social events. Working in the factory became a major part of my life every day after school, on weekends, and during summers from the time I was in the fifth grade until after I had graduated from Stamford High School and left home. For numerous reasons, I never enjoyed the work even though it was the one constant factor in my life throughout those eight years.

My participation in the business was fueled by duty and obligation, not desire or pleasure. My father's often invoked phrase, "Being good isn't good enough," seemed to place unnecessary pressure on a relationship that had always been distant at best and trying at worst. One recollection might offer some insight on the manner in which my work efforts were valued.

Throughout World War II few men were available to work, and my father needed someone to drive one of the delivery and installation trucks. At the age of fourteen, I was sent to the property in back of the shop, put in the driver's seat of a 1935 International truck, and given a short explanation of how the pedals and gears worked. My father then told me to practice by driving around the yard until the motor did not stall when I released the clutch. After a day or so I reported to him that I could drive. Later that week he evidently talked to the appropriate good old boys downtown and secured a driver's license for me. Thereafter, I was put on the road with an older man who was my helper. (Or I was his. I never knew for certain.) Regardless, he was usually too drunk to worry about our safety, yet his advice was ever present. You can imagine the two of us installing a spring-roller awning on the second or third floor of a hotel, each of us straddling and grasping an old wooden ladder with one hand and holding the awning with the other, as he performed a ballet on each rung. I surely had more to worry about than he.

Some say young children have a way of blocking reality when it is unpleasant, and they must be resilient to survive much of what they are exposed to. I feel certain I was no exception.

I: The Early Years (1927-1945)

My mother (born Carrie Stamer) died when I was fourteen. I discovered her lying on the kitchen floor when I came to eat breakfast before leaving for school. I called my father by phone, and from then on all was blank until I was awakened during the night a week later and brought to the hospital to kiss my unconscious mother goodbye. I am not certain whether I cried then, but I am sure I have not cried since. I loved my mother deeply and I believe she loved me, always protecting me from my father's verbal displays of dissatisfaction with me and with her as well, often at her expense. Perhaps this is why I remember few of the events that contributed to my youthful unhappiness from the time of her death in 1941 until I left home in 1945 when I was inducted into the U.S. Army. Also, I seem to have erased from my memory most of what came before her death. Of course, the aftermath of the 1929 stock market collapse and consequent Depression had permeated our daily lives and influenced my thoughts. Even when seeing the few photos I have of her, I only vaguely remember what she looked like. However, I can still imagine her feelings of warmth and concern.

In addition to running the awning business with a partner, my father, Martin, was a self-taught musician who in later years became the secretary and business agent of the Stamford Local 626, American Federation of Musicians. He played the saxophone and trumpet at routine events and any other opportunities that presented themselves. His two occupations allowed him to provide better for the family financially, though he was unhappy spending money. Had I participated in and succeeded in sports as my father had, we might have been closer. But I had no interest in athletics, none whatsoever. I was a loner, quite sensitive, and a keen observer who made few comments. Books were around the house, but I cannot remember ever reading one. Reading was not encouraged in my elementary school, which I believe was administered primarily by political appointees. Perhaps my mother was aware of the educational deficiencies in my school and that was why she played an active role in state and local parent-teacher organizations. At one time, she served as president of the Connecticut parent-teachers' organization.

My family owned and lived in what appears to me now to be a very small house, a duplex with upper and lower apartments, the latter of which was rented out. My two older sisters, Eleanor and Marilyn, and I slept in one of the two bedrooms. When I drive through Stamford to teach seminars in New England, I usually stop at the cemetery in New Canaan, Connecticut, where both my parents are buried. I can't explain why, but I always allow extra time to drive and walk around my childhood neighborhood, tracing the path back and forth to my elementary school. I associate so many inexplicable and unpleasant feelings with the area, yet I am compelled to return whenever possible. Perhaps this need exists because I know I'm no longer trapped there and can leave as soon as I please.

My parents did not keep a kosher home, but they were partial to kosher foods. We were Sephardic cultural Jews more than religious ones, certainly not of orthodox beliefs, though we observed some of the high holidays. I had my bar mitzvah at the typical age of thirteen, about a year before my mother died. Among the most vivid things about the occasion of "becoming a man" was the gift of a wristwatch from my parents. I suspect I am not an exception to the comment, cultural indoctrination notwithstanding, that a bar mitzvah may represent an honorable discharge from the religion.

Another recollection was the expected squabbling among aunts and uncles before and after the ceremony. Of his many siblings, I was acquainted with only one uncle and one aunt on my father's side.

At a young age I discovered I knew nothing of my ancestral roots, as all of my grandparents were deceased except my aged grandmother on my mother's side, Minnie, who died during my early teens. My father spoke sparingly about his mother and father, but he did tell me I was the namesake of his father, Elias Gordon. I know absolutely nothing about my great grandparents and their backgrounds other than my father's family had come to the United States from Russia and my mother's from Romania, sometime during the 1880s. I have always envied persons who have knowledge of several generations of their ancestors.

Although I do not care to dwell on the matter, my parent's marriage was not a happy one. My mother was a high school graduate and my father's formal education terminated with his completion of the fifth grade. She was born in 1896 in Brooklyn, New York, and he in Stamford in 1892. I suspect divorce in those days would have been a drastic step, and, moreover, I am not certain there was enough money to support two households. I have often theorized my mother's cerebral hemorrhage may have been caused by two forces, the stress in her personal life and the events leading up to World War II, including reports of the Holocaust. One can understand the threat Jewish people felt, considering their persecution in Europe. I can still hear the fear my mother's voice held when she talked to visiting relatives about the possibility of Hitler conquering the world and the subsequent fate of her children. I think it was too much for her to bear. Three weeks after the Japanese bombed Pearl Harbor, she was gone.

During my freshman year in high school, perhaps in rebellion against my mother's passing, I became friendly with a rowdy group of boys with whom I skipped school, drove "borrowed" family cars, and engaged in pranks throughout the city. I also had my first close encounters with young girls. Things were getting out of control, and as a consequence my father began to pay attention to me. He asked if I would like to play an instrument, and when I answered in the affirmative, he asked which one. I answered, "The big thing with strings that you stand up to play." I meant the string bass, and he quickly made the correct association. I had seen the instrument and was attracted to its tone quality and range in elementary school when I journeyed to the Metropolitan Opera House in New York City to see *Carmen*. My mother was one of the chaperones. In an attempt to direct my interest away from questionable activities, my father soon bought me a string bass and secured a local teacher who played the bass around town but whose primary instrument was the guitar. My weekly lessons began at age fifteen. They were my first serious exposure to music.

Sam, my teacher, had me draw long bows for a few weeks, and all the while I was squeezing a tennis ball with my left hand to acquire the necessary strength to press the strings against the fingerboard. In addition, I painfully stretched and separated the space between the first and second fingers of my left hand so the G-sharp to A on the G string and the D-sharp to E on the D string in the half position would be in tune. I don't remember having a method book, but Sam would notate simple exercises for me to practice. Thus, I was necessarily taught to count note values and to learn note names. To the best of my memory, I was never asked to sing or move my body. Lord knows I was certainly not coordinated.

Was I prepared to study a musical instrument? Not at all. To make the point, I will relate a poignant incident. Neither classroom nor instrumental music was taught in my elementary school until fifth grade. I would guess the majority of students were not given any music guidance or comprehensive music instruction at home, although I suppose we all heard the sound of music one way or another. My father never played his instruments at home. Nonetheless, the music specialist arrived sometime during the first few weeks of school. As fifth grade students, we were going to have a music class one period a week. How long the periods were I cannot recall, but to me they seemed an eternity. One of the flashbacks that remains etched in my psyche is the first day our music teacher appeared. She wore a wide-brimmed hat. Peering out the classroom window, I watched as she left school, and upon entering her car, she took out a long cigarette holder in which she placed a cigarette, lit it, and drove away. She smoked!

After a few music appreciation lessons, which included listening to some of the old standbys, such as "Anitra's Dance," we were told to come to the front of the room one by one and sing "The Battle Hymn of the Republic" solo as the teacher accompanied us at the piano. I remember the shock of the short piano introduction and then her glare as she kept shaking her head at me to indicate I should begin to sing. I sensed then and know now she must have pitched the song in a key only a castrato could have dealt with. I was silent as I watched and listened to her unanswered playing. As she performed for a captive audience, my embarrassment reached a zenith. My attempts at vocalization felt like an endless painful screech. It is needless to recount the displeasure and disdain of my new teacher, who immediately bestowed the label blackbird upon two or three of my male classmates and me. We were then told to sit in the rear of the room during every music period and to listen to the bluebirds sing. Although we were to appear as part of the class at assembly performances, we were instructed to only move our lips, not to make sounds. This continued until I left junior high school at the end of eighth grade and entered high school on the other side of town. I am sure it was a happy separation for both teacher and pupil. To this day, though I sing, I have never found my natural singing voice. Although it is steadily but slowly improving, my intonation is undependable at best and questionable at worst.

My early experience with my new companion, the string bass, was decidedly more positive. After a few months, Sam told my father I had progressed to a point where he could no longer teach me. Evidently no one else in town was up to the task, so I kept playing and teaching myself. The music teachers in high school were not aware of my newfound interest, and I made no attempt to convey that knowledge to them. Thus, I did not participate in traditional school music ensembles. As a senior, it became evident I played bass when I was asked to perform in the school orchestra, along with community musicians, for a performance of Verdi's *Requiem* in the high school auditorium. During my junior year I joined a dance band that played at school and community functions. We read stock arrangements, and I don't recall any of us attempting to improvise. Nonetheless, I was especially pleased when the notation consisted of only chord symbols, and I was successful in interpreting their meanings. In spite of these experiences, I was virtually at a standstill in my musical development, and I knew it. I heard other bass players doing innovative things on recordings, but I could not deduce a technique by which to accomplish them. I taught myself how to play pizzicato so I could play popular music, but, as I look back, I certainly made things difficult for myself.

While I was still in high school, an unexpected and influential happening took place. Bob Crane, later to be the star of the TV show *Hogan's Heroes*, was the drummer in the high school dance band, and we became inseparable. We used family cars to transport my bass and his drums to our engagements, always traveling together. During one ride, Bob remarked that he also needed a teacher and was getting frustrated because he didn't know how to improve his technique. It was his idea to skip school one day and take the New York, New Haven, and Hartford Railroad train to New York City in search of teachers. I readily agreed. It was only an hour's train ride and cost about a dollar or so round trip. We had the money, but were not sure what we would do upon arriving in the city. Nonetheless, we excitedly found ourselves standing somewhere on 52nd Street in Manhattan when Bob, who was infinitely more aggressive than I, spotted Teddy Wilson, Sid Weiss, a famous drummer whose name I cannot recall but who called everyone Face (because he could rarely remember names), and Benny Goodman emerging from a building. Bob immediately approached them, introduced himself, then me, and started a conversation. Goodman quickly left, but the others carried on a

I: The Early Years (1927-1945)

conversation and were gentle with us. I have since learned that the more secure persons are, the more humble and compassionate they tend to be. By the time the conversation ended, I had Sid Weiss's phone number and Bob had been directed to the Adler Drum Studio for lessons. Subsequently, I called Sid and arranged a meeting in New York City for a lesson. As it turned out, Sid had never taught, and that remained the case throughout his life. I became his one and only student.

At my father's request and with the school principal's permission, I left school early one afternoon each week so I could travel, sometimes with Bob, to the big city. My lessons took place at Sid's home on Long Island where his wife, Mae, treated me like one of her sons. After we all ate a late lunch, the lesson would begin. Sid would lie on the couch, whistle perhaps a Gershwin tune, and I would play a supportive bass line. He would ask why I did what I did, offer several alternatives, and we would try again until he was satisfied. That was my introduction to the contrapuntal harmonic technique of bass playing. He constantly reminded me, "Every note is going somewhere, even the last one." That is, I was to hear an additional note silently after the tune was over, so the actual final note of the song would be expressed musically. That may have been the wellspring of audiation (the ability to hear and to understand music without the physical sound necessarily being present), perhaps what the Italians refer to as *nota mentale*. Because Sid never had extended formal music instruction and was self-taught, most of my instruction was practical, in terms of making music without the complexities of theoretical explanations. He maintained an unencumbered style of interchange between us by using the simple terms "go up," "go down," or "change strings." We never discussed solos, as Sid insisted the primary purpose of a devoted bass player was to "lay down a respectable foundation for the musicians who were soloing." Throughout this time, Mae, in her inimitable lovely manner, became a surrogate mother. Later in life, a few years before Sid's passing, I conducted recorded interviews with him a few hours a day over a period of a week at his home in California. The cassettes, *Sid on Stage: A Glimpse of the Big Band Era*, have since been published by GIA.

One day, Sid said I should avail myself of "legitimate lessons." He had a teacher in mind, his friend Milton Kestenbaum, who was playing under Toscanini in the NBC Symphony. Sid arranged the details, and each week I had a lesson with Milton at Radio City Music Hall. When I arrived early enough and promised not to disturb the maestro, I was allowed to sit in Studio 8H and observe Toscanini rehearse the orchestra. On those occasions when I could understand what he was saying to the orchestra, I rightfully felt privileged. I learned so much simply by listening. For example, after the orchestra had finished tuning at a rehearsal, he asked, "The A sounds good gentlemen, but what about the B-flat?" Another time he said, "Pay attention to the piccolo note. The big notes take care of themselves."

Following my lesson with Milton, I would meet Sid and travel to Long Island for another lesson. Late in the evening, after dinner, I would make my way to Grand Central Station with my bass bow in a cover, a stick of resin, and a copy of Simandl Book I, and take the train back to Stamford. I used Sid's and Milton's basses when I had my lessons. I could hardly bear to return home and hear the sound of my own plywood instrument. In time, Milton sold me one of his basses, and it was the first time I owned a bass that was European and handmade. I was able to buy the bass using $500 left to me as the beneficiary of one of my mother's life insurance policies. The dual lessons lasted about two years, covering my final years of high school.

Evidently I was focused only on learning to play the string bass. Everything else paled by comparison. The last time I saw my high school transcript had to be more than fifty years ago, yet the grades remain imprinted in my mind. They were bad, very bad, and approximated a D average. I was advised by the school counselor not to even consider applying for admission to college. The thought of applying to the Eastman School of Music entered my mind, but, assuming I would return to Stamford and take over the awning works after my stint in the armed forces, my father did not encourage me in that direction. However, one of my close boyhood friends recently told me he was certain I applied and was accepted. That could be, but I have no recollection of the event.

Although I remember little of what took place during my conclusive years in high school, the bass remained my constant interest. I became more introverted, sensitive, and seemingly more insecure. I was attracted to several girls but was afraid to ask any of them on a date for fear of rejection. I know being Jewish and hearing many negative comments about it became a contributing factor to my inability to enjoy the little recognition I received as a musician. All other members of the high school dance band were Italian or Irish Catholics. As friendly as they were, I remained an outsider. They would talk among themselves about going to confession, and I was envious. Oh, if only I could have absolved myself of guilt as easily as they did. Guilt, the mainstay of being Jewish, in my father's words meant, "There is no forgiveness. Remorse stays with you as a reminder not to act foolishly again and not to ever forget that. The world expects more from a Jewish boy."

Throughout my high school years, I was given little direction at home. My father was interested in the business, my oldest sister, Eleanor, married shortly after my mother's death and followed her soldier husband from camp to camp until he was sent overseas before I graduated from high school. Marilyn, my other sister, was in her formative years and had her own life to lead. I know they cared for me, but I received nothing that could be considered motherly love or guidance from them. In the main, I learned to mostly fend for myself, cooking, laundering, and all.

As explained, I had little interest in schoolwork. The teachers seemed indifferent and the subject matter tedious. At school, there were two tracks: one for the college-bound and the other for the "non-academic" students. Ostensibly, because of my grades, I was inured to being shuffled into the latter group. There is no doubt I was bored, and I occupied most of my class time reading richly illustrated off-color magazines. Moreover, I developed a questionable relationship with a woman whose husband was serving overseas in the armed forces. Unfortunately, our association came to the attention of one of my sisters, who told my father. He insisted I put a stop to such activity as "it could lead to serious trouble." Consequently, in my senior year of high school my attention was forcefully shifted back to music.

Because of World War II, the shortage of mature musicians in the country club–saturated area of Fairfield County in Connecticut and Westchester County in New York was evident. Leaders of society bands from New York and the surrounding areas desperately needed musicians to fulfill their club-date commitments. I joined the musician's union and was hired to play with bands, such as Lester and Howard Lanin and Ben Cutler, who had booking offices in New York City, and several upscale bands from Stamford. I must say I hurriedly learned, through consultation with Sid, to be a professional bassist who could play a variety of show tunes, all in various keys without the aid of notation. As a result, in terms of improvisation, I was not a musical neophyte when I left high school and entered the Army.

II
Glimpse of the Future
(1945-1956)

I had just turned eighteen, and, of course, I was unfamiliar with Army life and the shouting of macho boot camp sergeants. I knew enough, however, not to let it be known I was a musician. Before I could assess what had happened to me and how my life had changed so drastically, I was getting up early, saluting everything that moved, saying, "Yes, sir," and being scolded more often than not. Even though my induction took place after Germany and Japan surrendered, occupational forces were still being sent overseas. Although I recall little of my childhood and my high school recollections are of my final two years, my memories are more lucid beginning with my military experience. Perhaps this was the first time in my life I was happy, but the beginning of that experience had all the earmarks of calamity.

When sent to Fort Leonard Wood in Missouri for basic training, I soon realized I didn't care for Army life at all. I had never handled a gun and felt most uncomfortable with one. I remember thinking I could never shoot anyone. What if I had to save my own life? I had no answer. Time would tell. I fulfilled the tasks of kitchen police (KP) and guard duty. I was getting along as well as could be expected until practice on the rifle range became an earnest matter. My comrades were being praised and receiving sharpshooter medals while I was constantly being reprimanded and embarrassed. The trouble was when I shot the rifle, using the designated trigger finger, that finger began to hurt and swell. I was worried I would damage my pizzicato playing, so I began using the middle finger as the trigger finger. Immediately I became a menace on the rifle range, but no one, not even the sergeant or second lieutenant in charge, took time to observe the problem. They assumed I was simply a terrible shot.

During practice one day I was told to leave the rifle range and report to company headquarters. I saluted the captain, and he returned the salute in exasperation. He then asked, "Soldier, what the hell did you do before joining the Army?" I told him I was a musician. Holding his hand over his eyes he said, "I should have known." I was told not to return to the rifle range again. Within a week, my group completed basic training and was being prepared to become part of an occupation force in Japan. Before I could contemplate the implications, I received special orders to report to Fitzsimmons General Hospital in Denver, Colorado, where I was to become a member of the 302nd Army Band. With a gun, I was a threat to my comrades; with a bass, that threat was neutralized. It goes without saying that everyone involved was relieved.

My membership in the 302nd Band represented a happy solution to an impossible situation. When I arrived in Denver, I was asked to play for the director of the band. He had been a bass drummer in World War I and remained in the Army as an enlisted man. With the outbreak of World War II, he was promoted in rank. I was informed I would be playing string bass in the concert band and at all affairs at the Officers' Club. However, there was a problem. I had no Military Occupation Status (MOS). The Army did not recognize string players, only musicians who could play a military band instrument. In order for me to remain with the band, I had to learn to play the tuba. Summarily, I was relegated to a small room with a tuba and a method book, and was told to teach myself to play tuba. In about three weeks, someone

II: Glimpse of the Future (1945-1956)

from Camp Lee in Virginia visited and tested me; I passed, and all was well. The possibility of failure did not enter my mind. Thereafter, I was expected to march in special parades and play retreat. Only the bugler was required to play reveille, so for the first time in months I was able to catch up on sleep.

I quickly discovered marching with a tuba wasn't easy. I read notation attached to a lyre as I marched, and I could see virtually nothing in front of me. On one occasion I stepped into a hole in the road and tripped while the band was being reviewed. One does not make a mistake like that twice. Having a clear vision of my marching path became far more important than misappropriating a few notes. It seemed my tuba playing was an evil to be endured by all if I were to play bass in the jazz groups. Performing informally became particularly pleasant after my bass arrived from home and I was able to play on a good instrument. The bass at the Officers' Club was a plywood Epiphone that emitted bowed sounds like those that might have emanated from ripping canvass in an empty oil drum.

I was relatively young, a blossoming musician surrounded by much older, more mature musicians. Some of the musicians, taking a special interest, allowed me to jam with them for hours each day. They taught me the chord progressions to many standard tunes, demonstrated all kinds of practices at the keyboard, and insisted that I behave like a bass player by playing "on top of the beat," not rushing, and yet always pushing the band and supporting the soloist. Some of the musicians had just returned from the European theater and were assigned to the 302nd while waiting to be discharged; they were eager to return to their professional careers. Some had played in the Glenn Miller Band, and others played under Ray McKinley's leadership after Glenn Miller was lost at sea. Words cannot express how much I learned from them about music and life in general.

The musicians in the band had nothing but disdain for the conductor. They liked the sergeant, who was his assistant, but they could not bear the commissioned officer. Unfortunately for him, the musicians relieved their frustration during our weekly concerts, either on or off the base. When the maestro began to conduct, it was prearranged that we would suddenly not play. He would stop conducting and look at us in confusion while a member of the band would give us four beats by pounding his heel on the floor, and we would begin playing. Then the director would start conducting, but he never knew for sure whether we would play or when we would stop playing. Sometimes we would observe the first ending, and sometimes not. Other times we would make a *da capo* without his direction. When he found his place and was sure the piece was destined to end, he would indicate a retard and stop conducting, but we would continue playing. Eventually, probably due to a nervous condition, he was relieved of his duties and a new officer took command. I am ashamed to admit I was a willing participant, too cowardly not to go along with the group. Perhaps the leader deserved it, because nothing infuriated the musicians more than when he would copy a stock arrangement, substitute the introduction for the first ending, then recopy it and claim it as his own. I am certain he meant well, and I remember him fondly.

A more significant occurrence for me was meeting a fellow in the band, slightly older than I, who became one of my few close friends. He had a profound influence in shaping my life. Hal Douthit had completed one year at Yale before he was drafted. He was appalled at my lack of education and limited vocabulary, but claimed he recognized my potential. Hal could not believe I didn't plan to attend college after leaving the service and took matters into his own hands. He reminded me I did not have to be dependent upon anyone for money because I would have the GI Bill to see me through at least two and a half years of college, and by that time other opportunities might present themselves. I liked Hal very much and respected his intellect.

II: Glimpse of the Future (1945-1956)

On a day of leave, Hal and I took the bus into Denver and found a bookstore. Without explanation, he purchased two copies of the same dictionary. We walked and talked for a while, and then returned to the base. The next morning, my tutoring was initiated. We sat at a table. Beginning with the A's, I read the first ten words on the page, recited the definitions of each word, and then used each word in a sentence. The following day, we took the next ten words in the order in which they appeared on the page, and we followed the same procedure. Hal sought others to engage me in conversation using the selected words. This process went on until Hal decided I had increased my vocabulary enough and would no longer embarrass myself or anyone else. About two months before we were both discharged from the Army, Hal presented me with an application for admission to the Eastman School of Music. He had sent for it without my knowledge, not knowing whether I had or had not applied at an earlier time. I would have been unable to give either an affirmative or negative answer with certainty even if he had posed the question. He reasoned that given my poor high school record, I could not expect admission to a good liberal arts school, but I had a chance of acceptance by a good music conservatory. Thus, we completed the application together, and Hal arranged for me to make a recording of my bass playing by having one member of the band play a piano accompaniment and another operate a recording machine. I think I played a transcribed Eccles sonata. Then my signed application and recording were sent to the registrar at Eastman.

Hal was right; I was accepted. Though I knew my classical playing was not outstanding, I believe the determining factor was that one of the Eastman orchestras needed another bass player. Although I sent back all of the required documents, I remember Hal's understandable doubt as to whether I would follow through and actually attend the school. As we parted, he lectured me about keeping my commitment. As I remember, my enlistment was up

May 13, 1947, and I left the Army a few days before he did. We had no contact until I arrived at Eastman, and he phoned me at the boarding house to make certain I had arrived in Rochester and matriculated. I did not hear from Hal for some time, although I attempted to locate him on several occasions. It was not until recently that Hal phoned me again. However, I doubt he will ever fully know how he changed my life, and the extent to which I am indebted to him. I have since thanked him and attempted to let him know I am aware of the significant role he played in shaping my future. However, he makes little of his benevolence, claiming he remembers none of the details.

Overall, my tenure at Eastman was not particularly pleasant. When I arrived there I was somewhat forlorn. I had been around, engaged in a lot of solitary thinking, met many types of persons of all ages, and did a lot of traveling with the Army band. Nonetheless, I felt out of my element in the current situation. For the most part the students were fairly sophisticated, upper middle class and higher, and Christian. Even Hal could not have prepared me socially for college. In a short time, I looked upon myself as a misfit, if not a pariah. I wanted to be accepted, but I was afraid of mingling and the possibility of rejection. I was attracted to some girls, but they did not want to be bothered with me. One of my personal shortcomings was that I was not exciting: I was not studying composition or conducting. At best, I was merely going to be a member of an orchestra and a bass player at that. I felt like a peasant among feudal lords.

To add to my inferiority complex I, like all conservatory students, began to compare my musicianship, in terms of my ability to audiate and my instrumental technique, to my classmates'. It was obvious I was far from being the best musician, though I was not the worst. This might have been the moment I took up the odious habit of exaggeration. My imagination had worked overtime trying to please relatives, particularly my father, who liked to brag about me and selfishly wanted me to be success-

II: Glimpse of the Future (1945-1956)

ful and so conferred upon me the misguided comfort of undeserved accomplishments. I knew full well what I was doing when I stretched the truth, but I continued doing it while courting the fear of embarrassment, concomitant with being discovered as a fabricator. What added to the difficulty was I tended to project what I thought persons were thinking and saying, twisting these thoughts to accommodate my desires, and then confusing them with reality. Even though I somewhat understood the psychology of the situation, I often took matters to extremes. It was not until my later years that I was able to begin to discard some of my unpleasant behavioral patterns. In time, I rarely felt the need to pretend I was someone other than myself.

What turned out to be most painful for me was society's failure to recognize prevailing anti-Semitism. At that time, it was not uncommon for many colleges and universities to practice quota systems where white Protestants were given preference in the admission and placement processes. Persons of Jewish birth and African Americans remained at the other end of the spectrum. Hearing someone casually make a caustic ethnic remark, even when he or she was aware of my background, made me extremely angry and uncomfortable. Should I speak up and destroy the social occasion, perhaps insuring I would not be welcome at future gatherings? This was a tough decision. After experiencing this situation several times, I found I was no wiser in solving the problem. Having been harassed as a child for being a "Christ killer" and being beaten by the town tough guys as I walked home from elementary school should have prepared me for later life. But there is a difference between being hurt physically and being damaged psychologically. To this day I find I am still sensitive about the matter, though perhaps less emotional.

More and more I became a loner. My small circle of friends included a few jazz musicians, such as Ray Shiner, whose boundless humor and uncanny sarcasm was all I needed to see me through some of my low periods. He didn't care about things other than whether a person was able to swing and improvise. I played regularly with Carl Dengler's band, working long hours and making enough money to get by with dignity while maintaining my musical integrity, even though I had to read arrangements. If my bass line did not duplicate that of the pianist's left hand, I was in trouble with Carl.

There was also an African American violist, Al Brown, who became a rather close acquaintance. I remember offering him a ride to New York City when I returned to Stamford for Christmas vacation. He also experienced feelings of being an outcast. Neither of us was invited to become a member of the coveted music fraternity at Eastman. Some of the members had girlfriends who appeared to be products of a finishing school rather than students attending a music conservatory. Ironically, it was not until I became a professor at the University of Iowa and because of my growing reputation and acknowledged academic status that a school administrator insisted I actually participate in the ceremony of joining that fraternity. Though I am a life member, for all intents and purposes I am inactive. If it were possible to recapture the past, I probably would not have joined the group.

Being Jewish was and still is an influential part of my life. I can't imagine how different my life might be had I not indirectly absorbed Jewish culture, not the least of which is the importance of work, education, art, and motivation (not ambition) to be the best. So many times I was told by my father, "It is not the clothes you wear that makes others respect you and be nice to you, it is how you are able to use your mind to meet whatever their needs may be." It is unfortunate nature does not allow one the opportunity to compare the achievement of a controlled experiment to an actual life experience.

During my first year at Eastman, I attended classes and practiced as expected. Sometimes I remained in a practice room

II: Glimpse of the Future (1945-1956)

more than five hours a day, concentrating on difficult orchestral passages for the double bass, transcribed solos, and etudes. Actually, I had no idea why I was told to practice or how to practice. That is, I did not have the good sense to direct myself to listen to orchestral literature so I would have a clue as to what the passages were supposed to sound like, at least in terms of tempo. What a travesty no one seemed aware that it is not the amount of time devoted to practice, but rather the quality of time spent practicing that is important. Further, the faculty was probably not familiar with research indicating that distributed practice was much more valuable than massed practice, meaning several short periods of practice yield much greater results than one long practice period. I suspect any concept related to audiation was far from their understanding. Moreover, had they been presented with the idea of adapting instruction to students' individual musical differences, it probably would have been viewed as a remote, if not a strange notion.

My applied music teachers seemed not to know when giving lessons that two instruments must be reckoned with, the actual instrument and the audiation instrument. It was obvious developing instrumental technique was their major concern. I was receiving good grades in my academic classes but knew I wasn't progressing as I should with my instrumental performance. Specifically, I was having technical problems I didn't know how to solve. One teacher was of particularly sparse help, often stating he did not enjoy teaching. When I asked a question relating to technique, he would reluctantly rise from his chair, shift his cigarette in his mouth, take the instrument, and demonstrate so quickly I had no idea what he was doing. He would then take his seat, speak (not sing) solfege, and look out the window again. I was intimidated. He rarely said anything except to tell me I was playing the wrong note, which in most cases I already knew. In short, because, among other things, I was not a great student, teachers showered whatever favors they could on those who were more promising and obliging. I received neither encouragement nor assistance in finding playing opportunities. Such favor and compassion were reserved for other students.

I am by no means trying to blame others for my lack of music aptitude or music achievement. However, I must say I wish I had been asked to leave the school or given assistance in learning to the degree my potential would have allowed. Neither option was forthcoming. I can distinctly remember my frustration in moving in what seemed like a never-ending circle. One day, I decided as all else had failed, I must try to become my own teacher. I suspected my intonation was less than to be desired, but was at a loss to know what to do about it. Finally, I came to the conclusion if I sang what I was trying to play, perhaps I could reconcile the discrepancy and improve my playing. I was of the opinion my rhythm was not a problem, while my intonation had always been unreliable.

To be sure, I am not attempting to wax philosophically and suggest that all bad situations have a purpose and they ultimately lead to something beneficial not ascertainable at the time. Albeit, I sought help from a voice teacher and in a matter of a lesson or two found a singing voice. It was not my natural voice. That has yet to be found, but I could sing *mezzo voce* (in a half voice), not falsetto. I believe as a result of the intolerable situation I found myself in I became curious and my research instinct came to the fore. Furthermore, I became conscious of the necessity of audiation. I was not yet motivated to attempt to give it a name or describe it even though a semblance of it proved essential in dealing with my initial struggles.

At this stage of musical development, my singing voice was so bad there was no way it could help my intonation in playing the bass. I would not be surprised to learn now that it restricted my progress. Regardless, I kept practicing and made little improvement. Why I remained at Eastman and did not leave on my own

II: Glimpse of the Future (1945-1956)

volition, I am not certain, but I can venture a guess. I evidently reasoned even though performance stardom was not in my future, if I could eventually earn a degree from a school with a good reputation, it would possibly compensate for my limitations and eventually assist me in allied professional pursuits. Further, I concluded, if it takes a school twenty-five years to gain a reputation, it should take at least fifty years to lose it, and I would be able to use my degree to enjoy some professional success before time ran out. I certainly did not want to return to the Stamford Awning Works, but I also knew I had to come up with something challenging and worthy of pursuit. My GI benefits were to run out in the middle of my junior year, and I had to make some progress.

Unbelievably, by the end of my freshman year I received an A in string bass following the B at midyear. Was I really learning and improving? Who was I to say? True, I had no social life. Because I played many dance jobs at country clubs and debutante parties, it was necessary to buy an old car in order to travel to my places of work, and my father contributed some money to make that possible. After the first semester of my freshman year I moved and boarded with a rather elderly couple, the Esterman's. With the exception of the musicians I worked with, I led a solitary life. I knew other students at school, but I had only one or two friends in the true sense of the word. I was self-reliant in every way. Even now, I feel pain and empathy for the young man I was at the time.

Not knowing what else to do, I returned to Eastman for my sophomore year. As with any decision, the outcome was not all good or all bad. Perhaps the manner in which an angel could have been looking over my shoulder and guiding me was not meant for mortal understanding. However, one thing I can say with conviction is that had I not returned, I would not have my three lovely daughters, and for them I am most grateful.

Sometime during my sophomore year, 1948–49, I met a student who entered Eastman the year before I did. She seemed to know her way around, and for reasons I was too naive to understand at the time, she sought me out. It was easy for her to do, as we were often in adjacent practice rooms. Nothing can be gained from all the details, but to state it simply (and certainly not at my insistence), we were married April 1949. Because of my insecurity and the attention she paid me, I was flattered and thus, allowed myself to be led into this obliged union. Moreover, as I look back on the situation, perhaps I thought I was marrying a family. As I have intimated, I never felt had a family, and I thought hers was an intact happy one. I remember thinking I might recapture my mother in her mother. Of course, reality did not allow things to work out that way. Although it may seem unbelievable, I did not love the woman I was about to marry. Nonetheless, I went through with the wedding, a ceremony in her home at which both a rabbi and a minister officiated, neither displaying any more happiness than I, but both families looking on with cautious hope.

Although I did not love her, I think I liked her. However, within the first week of marriage, as a result of comments overheard in the men's locker room and later through conversation with her, I no longer even liked her because of her evident lack of forthrightness. We lived together in a small apartment, but I tried to separate myself physically as well as psychologically from her as much as possible. I had no idea what was going on in her mind, but she soon dropped out of school and began to work as a secretary. I was of the opinion that she was eager to leave school, and marriage offered her an excellent opportunity to satisfy her wish.

We were divorced some twenty years later when I was a professor at the University of Iowa. During that time span, I suffered alternating pains of guilt and anger, but life went on. I could not help but wonder then, and I still wonder today, why I remained in the marriage. Nonetheless, I was unconsciously preoccupied with preparing myself professionally, but was unaware of why or how

II: Glimpse of the Future (1945-1956)

that was happening. When I sculpt, I tend to follow the grain of the wood, and I was similarly living then, simply following one experience after another and letting the sequence of events determine the course. Although I was the main character in the tale, I was not in command.

Given the circumstances of my marriage and the dissatisfaction I felt over my progress in bass performance, I needed a change. Also, my GI money was about to evaporate at the end of the first semester of my junior year, and it was obvious I could not support my wife and myself and still attend school. The dance jobs were plentiful, but I could not work late in the evenings and manage to keep my academic commitments. In spite of frequent but futile arguments with the head of the music theory department over the idea that common practice music theory had nothing do with the theory of music, only with an explanation of music notation, or that the augmented fourth is not the most difficult interval to hear when it is audiated in a context other than major tonality (for example, lydian), I was able to keep abreast of classroom obligations. Nonetheless, I could not continue to live the life of a practicing jazz/commercial bassist while unrealistically hoping to become a respectable orchestral bassist. One style of playing melded into the other, and thus, I felt I wasn't really very good at either. One of my major teachers was not shy about reinforcing that idea. With that, I left Rochester with my wife, my bass, and what few belongings we had to seek whatever employment I could as a musician.

The Edwin Gordon who had arrived in Rochester two and a half years before and the Edwin Gordon leaving Rochester were far different persons. Although my fundamental personality did not change, I became somewhat broader in my thinking, but not in my behavior. I was still highly introspective, a non-conformist, very sensitive, and beginning to enjoy my own company. I became more committed to not becoming one of the crowd under any condition. This is not to say I would not have welcomed the friendship of those who engaged in thoughtful discourse, but they were hard to come by. I sought the company of older students and faculty, but there was little reciprocation. Consequently, I learned to rely on myself for topics to think about, and from this to develop some small level of sophistication.

If I was successful to any degree in this pursuit, I thank the American literature teacher I had at Eastman, Ethel Mae Haave. Throughout my freshman and sophomore years, I had been enrolled only in music courses. In the first semester of my junior year I registered for her course. I thoroughly enjoyed it. Ms. Haave, who I believe served as a part-time faculty member while pursuing a doctorate at Yale, suggested I read books beyond those required for the course. Then she would graciously meet with me and discuss the treatises, offering guidance and insight into the ideas contained in the works. I took comfort in knowing persons unknown to me, even if they were fictitious ones, shared my sense of isolation. Just to know they existed and might understand me and my thoughts helped me to maintain an optimistic outlook. I read Faulkner, Hemingway, T. S. Eliot, Emerson, Thoreau, Hawthorne, Melville, and others. At this time I discovered transcendentalism, and it seemed to be what I needed at the time. Ms. Haave spoke confidentially to me, suggesting I give up the idea of a music degree and move into the liberal arts, and, ultimately, into a profession where my success was not dependent upon working with others. Perhaps she saw in me what Hal did. For whatever reason, I did not heed her advice, and she did not force the issue.

I left Eastman feeling very much alone, but not lonely. Escaping from such a competitive and otherwise unhealthy environment was a relief. I took Emerson's essays seriously and became more self-reliant. I believe my mystical beliefs took hold at this time, and I must confess they have never totally left my consciousness. Despite my insecurity, I gained a sense of self-worth I cannot explain. My Jewish culture insisted I persist, and there

II: Glimpse of the Future (1945–1956)

was always hope. A mystic with a Jewish upbringing is no one to trifle with. Apparently some of my teachers were not aware of that.

My younger sister, Marilyn, and her husband, Reed Parker, a graduate student at Columbia University, were living in New York City. My wife and I decided to take a large apartment with them, share the costs, and pursue our separate fortunes. Because I maintained my membership in the musician's union in Stamford, I was able to obtain a transfer to Local 802 in New York City. Doing so allowed me to work single engagements for six months until I was able to apply for full membership in the New York City local and thus accept any type of position I was offered. I mingled with other musicians in the union building and ultimately was hired by some bandleaders for society jobs. I played continuous music, primarily show tunes with a "businessman's bounce," from nine in the evening until two in the morning with infrequent breaks. I never sought employment that made use of what I had supposedly learned (referred to as legitimate music) at Eastman. I usually had afternoons free, so I walked from 48th to 52nd streets looking for "Musicians Wanted" notices.

One day I saw such a sign, took the subway home to get my bass, and returned to what I remember as the Nola Studios. I carried the bass up four flights of stairs and waited in the anteroom alone. Soon someone entered and invited me inside to join a drummer and a pianist. I took the cover off my bass, did not take the time to tune the instrument, and immediately accompanied them in what they had begun to play. I don't remember the tune. The pianist asked, "Do you know rhythm?" I was not sure what I was being asked, but I nodded. Soon I recognized "I Got Rhythm." After a few choruses the drummer got up and left the room. Within a minute or so a rather small fellow came in, sat at the drums, and called a tune. We played it and a few more. Then he asked me, "How much do you want?"

"For what?"

"To travel."

"Where?"

"On the road by bus."

"With whom?"

"With me." The conversation ended abruptly when I was astonished to discover I was speaking to Gene Krupa, one of my boyhood idols.

I was so shocked I really don't remember how the conversation continued, except that I was hired for $170 a week on a guaranteed basis. My travel costs were covered, but I had to buy my own food and pay for a hotel if and when it was not necessary to travel by bus immediately to the next engagement. To the best of my recollection, I usually cleared more than $100 a week. I later learned some members of the band were paid on a *pro rata* basis; that is, they were paid according to how many nights per week they worked. I was expected to perform six nights a week, and if additional work were available, I was given extra pay. The fact is, I was so grateful to have the opportunity to work beside and learn from someone of Krupa's genius I would have accepted the job under any conditions. We generally played one-nighters and theaters.

I can say unequivocally that being a member of the Krupa band in 1950 was a true highlight of my life. I learned so much from Gene, particularly about rhythm. He was a generous, goodhearted man. When he was in the right frame of mind, he would talk to me and express his ideas about music. I do not doubt my theories of rhythm have their basis in Krupa's ideas. For example, what I refer to as macrobeats and microbeats, he referred to as big beats and small beats. However, more importantly, he insisted I feel both underlying beats as I played "the rhythm." He was undoubtedly suggesting I audiate macrobeats and microbeats as a foundation for performing rhythm patterns. The macrobeats established tempo, and the microbeats established meter. The rhythm itself is what "swung." He would often say, "I'm paying you to feel you, not to hear you. I can hire a loud bass player for a lot less than I'm paying you." Other times he would give me a sideglance if I was not moving as I played. He knew by the sound I was producing, without seeing me, when I was fatigued or my mind was wandering. That is not to say he wanted me to move to a beat, but to move between the beats. As my fingers maintained the rhythm, he wanted me to flow in continuous whole-body movement.

Although I cannot be sure, because he would never directly talk about it, I suspect he was not a schooled musician. He was able to read drum parts, but his tonal skills were limited. As a matter of fact, the lead alto saxophone player usually rehearsed the band as Krupa listened and the band boy played drums. After one or two times through, Krupa would go to the drums and play with the band. I doubt he ever actually read the notation for the tune. I know he didn't trust persons who were dependent on notation. On one occasion I heard him say to one of the sidemen, "I have enough aggravation on this band without you always reading." For his part, once or twice through the notation should have been sufficient: "The music isn't in the notes, it's in the ears and the body." Though he never expressed it as such, I feel certain he understood that the most important parts of music, particularly expression and phrasing, defy precise notation. In my opinion, notation explains nothing; it only assists one in remembering what has been already audiated. At best, notation is a window seen through that guides a musician in making music on the other side.

I was the youngest member of the band, and I felt Gene induced a distance between the others and me, perhaps because of the negative influences some might have on me. He did not want to feel responsible or be blamed for my becoming dependent on any type of undesirable substance. Thus, although I always felt comfortable near Gene, I didn't have a close friend in the band, except the female vocalist whose name I think was Dowdie O'Neill. She may have felt sorry for me. I was not a drinker, and I had no use for any type of drugs. Others were and did.

Krupa was aware I had attended a school of music and received some formal music instruction. For that reason, he rarely used my name, usually referring to me as "hey, professor." He would amuse himself by asking me revealing questions, such as "Why do you guys have so many numbers that all mean the same thing?" He was referring to enrhythmic measure signatures, the same-sounding rhythms that are notated differently, such as 3/4 and 6/8, 2/4 and 2/2, and 2/4 and 4/4. More than once I was reminded of the story about the Russian communist bureaucracy that paid musicians according to the number of measures they composed and/or transcribed. Thus, what might have been initially in 4/4 was changed to 2/4, or from 6/8 to 3/8 or 3/4, and no one appeared to know the difference. Gene forced me to soul search about the amount of "extra luggage schooled musicians carry around and burden others with as they perform and teach."

Most of the time I played what was notated, having committed to memory almost the entire library. I was given freedom, with restrictions, to add or change some notes as I saw fit as long as the rhythm wasn't compromised. I missed having opportunities to improvise, as I can't remember anyone in the band gathering after hours to play for their own gratification. I think we were perpetually weary from continuous night travel by bus. Typically, Gene was on the bus with us, but he slept most of the time.

How I came to leave the band may be of some interest. I was getting tired and becoming bored without extra-musical elements in my life. I had no one to talk to about anything other than music or what one might expect a group of solitary men to exchange thoughts about. I needed time to recuperate and digest what I had learned from Gene. Also, members of my family in Stamford, with whom my wife was living while I was traveling, were systematically

II: Glimpse of the Future (1945-1956)

writing and telling me my responsibility was to be at home with my wife. Her mother in Indiana also joined the chorus with cryptic written remarks. I know I was unsure of myself, but I must have also been craven to let others influence me and ostensibly direct my life. Gene ultimately suggested I leave the band.

The band usually traveled by bus. But on one occasion we were in Pittsburgh, Pennsylvania, and we had to perform at an Army Air Force base in St. Louis the next day. As I remember, the government provided a plane for us, and we flew. Once on the plane, the marijuana smoke became thick, and I had no choice but to inhale some of the blue cloud. The following day and evening I seemed to be unusually relaxed and experienced a carefree feeling that carried over into my playing. Although it was probably purely psychological, I projected the euphoria of second-hand smoke and decided to send the band boy for some marijuana and rolling paper so I could experience the glory firsthand. The messenger went directly to Krupa and reported my request. With that, Gene held up two fingers, which meant I was put on two weeks notice with pay. That was the union rule when a sideman's employment was terminated. At the end of the evening, the manager gave me my two weeks salary and we all said our good-byes. Not being terribly upset, I took my bass with me in a cab to the railroad station and headed for Stamford. I didn't feel any animosity and neither did Gene. We kept in touch until his death in the 1970s.

I didn't fully realize it then, but a very important part of my life and development as a musician and independent thinker had ended. How much more I could have learned from Gene about life and music, I will never know. I will always be indebted to him for his kindness and concern. Soon after I left, his big band broke up and he put together a small group. Whether he would have invited me to be a member of that ensemble I do not know, but if he had, I would have had an opportunity to improvise with some jazz greats. The small group did not stay together very long because Gene reunited with Benny Goodman on a European tour.

When I arrived back in Stamford, I worked local dance jobs, but they did not provide enough money for my wife and me to live decently. I don't remember the precise chronology of events before I returned to Eastman in time for the beginning of the 1951–52 school year. As I recall, I tried several things. I received a scholarship to study music at the University of Miami in Coral Gables, Florida, but was unhappy there and left after a few months. I also tried a well-established liberal arts school, Kenyon College in Gambier, Ohio, where I was given a tuition scholarship but soon discovered the situation did not meet my expectations. In desperation, I took a job as a management trainee at Bloomingdales department store. I was required to travel by train five days a week to New York City and quickly tired of that activity. Everyone in the business was in pursuit of money, and if I thought the students at Eastman were competitive, they could not begin to compare to the rising young cadre of ambitious executives in retailing.

I went back and forth from Stamford to New York where I played with society bands and did studio work. Gene helped me make advantageous connections, but I was beginning to sense the limitations of working in commercial music. It was no longer an option for two main reasons. First, jazz as I knew it was on the way out. It was being replaced by bebop and the emerging styles of rock-and-roll. Try as I might, like many musicians far more capable than I, I could not make the transition. I knew I was one of the "moldy figs," as the new generation of jazz artists referred to us. In time, I would have no work because I could not keep up with the tide of change, nor could I compensate for my lack of musicianship by being political. That was not in my genetic makeup.

Second, even if I were as good as I hoped I might be, I was not a good soloist. Thanks to Sid's tutoring, I played an acceptable contrapuntal harmonic bass line as support for the front-line artists,

II: Glimpse of the Future (1945-1956)

but it was embarrassing to listen to my solos. I took jobs with the understanding I would not be asked to do solos. This proved limiting, as the role of the bass was gradually becoming a solo instrument in jazz. Its more mundane role as a harmonic/rhythm instrument was becoming passé. I knew time was running out for me. When I received a letter from Eastman inquiring about my intentions to return to school (I had requested a leave of absence) with an offer of financial assistance that would see me through the completion of a bachelor's degree in music, I immediately grasped the opportunity. Though it may not seem to have been the wisest choice, logically speaking, I literally had no alternatives. Rochester offered me far more opportunities than Stamford, and at that time who knew what surprises the future had in store? The positives outweighed the negatives. However, I did know in my heart I would not perform as a professional jazz or classical bassist as a vocation. I would need to find options that would allow me to make use of my music background.

Having worked with Krupa, I returned to Eastman as a hero among students. However, many of the faculty looked upon that experience with disdain; if anything, it tainted me as not being a serious musician. Taking that in stride, I attended one or two sessions of summer school and received a bachelor's degree in music in string bass performance in 1952. I can't remember anything momentous happening during that period. In addition to my studies, I worked six nights a week at the Triton Supper Club, and my wife worked as a secretary. We had enough money to live modestly.

Quite predictably, I didn't know what to do after graduation. It seemed the only avenue available to me was to join a second- or third-tier symphony orchestra. I didn't want to play jazz and go back on the road. In addition to not liking night traveling, I knew I could easily succumb to the enticement of addiction to soften the anticipated boredom and physical pain. When all else failed, I decided, as many young undergraduate students do today, to enter graduate school. I postponed the inevitable. I received a scholarship and then my master's degree in string bass performance and music literature from Eastman one year later in 1953.

The summer months after my undergraduate graduation and before graduate school were spent at my wife's parents' farm home in rural Indiana. Laboring at the awning works during the day and traveling to New York at night to work as a musician did not appeal to me. Thus, I sold Fuller brushes from door to door in several small Indiana communities and earned a sufficient sum of money to sustain me through my year of graduate studies. I even won several prizes for selling over a specified dollar amount of brushes in a given week. It wasn't difficult to reach the quota because the products are so good. I still use the clothes brush I purchased for myself at that time. Furthermore, I enjoyed meeting and talking to humble persons who made no pretense of being important.

Being somewhat more adult and a little more conciliatory in my behavior, I managed to get along better with my peers and the faculty in graduate school. Among other activities, I enjoyed playing solo bass in the Eastman Little Symphony under the direction of Frederick Fennell, who was one of the better musicians in the institution. He was benevolent and knowledgeable and would often offer me valuable musical advice. Playing Bach, Haydn, and Mozart was a welcome relief from performing many of the romantic compositions of Howard Hanson and other composers of a similar style whose music constituted the basic repertoire in senior symphony.

At the time, my required music theory courses centered on part-writing in the style of Bach. Throughout this instruction, if I used the two-seven sharp-four chord more than a certain percentage of the time, based on McHose's analysis of Bach's usage of that chord in the entire collection of Bach chorales, my grade

II: Glimpse of the Future (1945-1956)

was lowered. As a musician, that neither pleased nor made sense to me. I wanted to go beyond that type of instruction and study more about Mozart, but it would have necessitated adding an elective (if indeed one was being offered), and my schedule was always too full to add an extra course.

After leaving Eastman, I felt musically deprived. I have little doubt my overall exposure to music theory in school, coupled with Gene's incisive observations, marked the beginning of my life as a critic of the academic common practice music theory establishment. I would be remiss, however, not to mention the importance of having been exposed to the McHose-Tibbs rhythm syllables in music theory classes, which later proved to have a profound influence on my research, teaching, and publications. Nonetheless, in my opinion, music theory had, and still has, an unjustified stranglehold on the requirements sanctioned by the National Association of Schools of Music. As Jaques-Dalcroze pointed out more than 150 years ago, it would be far better for students to learn to move their body expressively and artistically as a prerequisite for all types of music instruction than to sit and write notation most of them appeared to be unable to audiate.

How many music majors among us have learned to spell German, French, and Italian sixth chords in every conceivable key. I had to do it in G-sharp and F-flat for my graduate orals, but I had difficulty distinguishing among them, let alone recognizing or identifying any one of them when hearing them performed. Notation, not audiation, captures the fancy of music theorists. After all, it is much easier to teach students to write something than to audiate it, even if the teacher might audiate. There is a difference between having something to teach and having to teach something.

Close to graduation, I volunteered to take two or three auditions for positions in minor symphony orchestras. The conductors were hearing students play in the Eastman Theater. I know I was offered one job, perhaps two, but in my heart I knew that playing bass in a symphony orchestra was not what I wanted to do. Still, I was not clear about what I did want to do. After the freedom I experienced when playing professional jazz, I could not envision working under what I considered to be a dictatorial conductor. I found playing bass in an orchestra boring, just doing what I was told by either the conductor or the notation. I wanted to believe I had marked my last bowing indications in the notation of familiar music I no longer wanted to hear myself or anyone else perform.

From Rochester I went directly to New York, and I had no choice but to be a commercial bassist until something better came along. Again, I played society jobs, and in addition I played some record dates. Also, I got on the Broadway show circuit and became a part-time pit orchestra musician. The most enjoyable part of show work was reading the personal and professional comments written on the pages of notation by bass players who had previously performed the music. I learned about conductors I had never met. It provided a living, but I was restless. I knew life had to have something better to offer. Because I persisted in thinking and searching, my future took a new direction when I met Philip Sklar, the principal bass player in the NBC Symphony under Toscanini. Phil was as an exceptional human being, an extraordinary musician and bass player. This is how it happened.

More and more I felt myself becoming depressed over my professional life. Although I was still certain I did not want to spend my life playing bass, I simply could not allow myself to become a robot performer and not see some improvement in my playing. I had to do something. Fortunately, I overheard in conversation Philip Sklar's name mentioned as a fine bass player and teacher. With some help, I found his name in the union telephone directory and called him. After a few calls and attempts to find a time convenient for both of us, I was invited to his home on Long Island, a relatively short subway and elevated train ride

II: Glimpse of the Future (1945-1956)

from Manhattan. When I arrived, Phil and his wife greeted me warmly. I immediately proceeded to the basement where Phil gave lessons and repaired basses. He was an excellent craftsman, and I can remember I was fascinated by the unique way he fitted a bridge, continually adjusting the sound post relative to the bass bar to attain the fullest sound.

I can't help but re-experience the trauma I felt when he asked me to play the piece I had prepared for him. I knew I was not a musician of the quality he was accustomed to hearing, but I played anyway, conjuring confidence by telling myself I was there for instruction. I wasn't more than two minutes into the first movement of the Dragonetti concerto, one of the pieces I had performed for my master's degree recital at Eastman, when he asked me to stop. Very quietly I was asked to play a one-octave B-flat scale. I started to do so, but he stopped me before I got to the second pitch. He posed various questions about why I was doing several technical things. He even asked me if I was physically comfortable holding the bass, and if I looked upon the bass as a good friend, if not a lover. The remainder of the lesson was spent playing the B-flat scale, descending rather than ascending, as I had originally intended to play it. The emphasis was not so much on intonation as it was on making the scale sound like a piece of music expressively performed. He stressed vibrato and dynamics, and, like Sid before him, reminded me every note had to be going somewhere. If even one note were static, there could be no music.

When I asked how much I owed him for the lesson and he responded, I must have looked shocked because he told me to pay him later after I had more lessons. I realized I had no choice. I was not carrying enough money to pay him, which also attests to my naiveté and lack of sophistication at that time. He sensed my immaturity and was gracious about it. I was certainly very ill at ease, because I can't remember how our meeting ended or how we made an appointment for the next lesson. However, I do recall as I was walking to the door, he put his hand on my shoulder and said, "Please, think about what you are going to play, and before you play it, think about it some more. Don't be in such a hurry."

The lessons continued for more than a year, and, as a result, life became tolerable for me. I was learning so much. The fact is Phil actually became a surrogate father to me. Phil, a Russian Jew, was educated in the Leningrad Conservatory. Our time spent together had less to do with music than with philosophy, religion, and the state of the world and my role in it. That is not to say I didn't play the bass. I did, and I also sang what I played and physically moved to the rhythm of what I was to play without holding the bass. We occasionally danced together. However, in my heart I knew he was not satisfied with my progress and felt somewhat frustrated about how to guide me. I seemed unable to learn some things, but he was not specific about the nature of the problems. In his own unassuming way, he continuously attempted to correct them. Nevertheless, he never wavered from telling me in spite of my preferences or thoughts about the matter that he was preparing me to be an orchestral bass player, and a good one at that. He was a genetic optimist.

Phil's efforts were unrelenting. I picked up on his words of wisdom, some reminiscent of Toscanini's: "You must always be hearing where the piece will end, the tonic, as you are performing, no matter what note you are playing. That is the way you play in tune"; "The most important part of music takes place between the beats, not on the beats. The big beats take care of themselves, so at most make a decrescendo, never a crescendo, except for a special effect"; "Tell me a story about what you are playing without talking. We may not agree, but tell me anyway." Soon I was visiting his home twice a week, often listening to and observing him give lessons to other students. After the student departed, he asked me if I approved of the way he explained

II: Glimpse of the Future (1945-1956)

something or if he might have expressed it better. He also wanted to know if a correspondence existed between his explanations and demonstrations. I can't be sure, but he might have assumed I had an analytical mind. Or he could have thought if I watched someone else being taught, I might absorb what he had to teach better than just hearing it once from him.

He stopped charging me for lessons, saying my observations and comments were valuable to him and they sufficed as payment. Whether he actually believed that or he had empathy for my plight as a musician without steady work, I will never know. We certainly had a tenderness for each other, and it was a pleasure to have a bass teacher who was a gentle soul. I would be remiss not to mention his wife, Ann, who was as generous and kind to me as Mae Weiss had been. With their penetrating perceptions, they both seemed to understand me.

As an aside, it might be of interest to know I tried on several occasions to get Philip Sklar and Gene Krupa to meet. I was curious as to how they would accept each other and, if Gene were in the right state of mind to participate, what they would talk about. I thought I might record the conversation and listen to it over and over again to ascertain worthwhile gems. They both were such fine musicians, yet they differed in many ways. Above all, I believe Gene probably felt insecure about his lack of formal music instruction, particularly when compared to Phil's background, and Phil had little use for jazz and famous jazz musicians who he said made so much money. Phil had no possible way to ever understand jazz, let alone play it. It just wasn't in him. Suffice it to say they both agreed to the meeting, each knowing realistically it would never take place. Their attitudes signaled to me I should cease pressing the matter.

On one memorable day, I arrived for my lesson and Phil, not Ann as was the usual custom, opened the door. Phil announced he was a little under the weather and did not want to teach that day, so in order to compensate me for my "wasted time" traveling to his home, he would like to take me to lunch. Without entering the house, we were off to a neighborhood Chinese restaurant. After ordering, Phil said he had something to tell me. Straight out, without hesitation or evident sympathy, he told me he knew whatever I did, I had to be the best, if not better than the best. He went on to say I could not attain that status through bass playing, because my playing was not good enough to secure a principal position in one of the four or five major symphony orchestras. As I had always suspected the main problem was my lack of good intonation. "What a shame," he said. "You are so rhythmical and expressive, but wanting in pitch."

My unspoken response was to ask myself the question, what do I do now? Before I could even try to mask what must have been a contorted facial expression, let alone deal rationally with the problem at hand, I realized Phil was speaking. Not to worry. He said he had taken care of everything. The plan he devised and the rationale behind it was this. Although I was not a great musician, I was a very good one. Moreover, I was highly intelligent, sensitive, and compassionate. Also, I had the ability to probe problems and devise realistic solutions. Because many music teachers in the public schools lacked a good share of those qualities, I should become a music educator. The point was, I was needed in the public arena, and I could be the best of the best there. Who knows, I might even become a leader in the profession. He took time to convince me of what he had to say, not knowing I didn't need any convincing because I would have done whatever he told me to do without question or reservation. He then announced we were going to a bass recital downtown. He mentioned the name of the performer, one whose playing I knew he abhorred. When I asked why were going, he quickly replied, "When you listen to someone who plays very well, it goes by so fast you can't learn anything. When you listen to someone who

II: Glimpse of the Future (1945-1956)

plays poorly, however, you can easily learn what not to do."

Phil knew I had not taken any music education courses at Eastman, and in order to teach in the public schools, I had to be certified. Thus, he arranged two things. First, I was to attend the State Teachers College in Danbury, Connecticut, that semester, enroll late, and take a methods course in classroom music with Elizabeth Dominy, a superb educator. When I completed that, I was to leave immediately for Ohio University in Athens, Ohio, and pursue a second master's degree in professional education. As part of that graduate program, I could make up whatever undergraduate courses were necessary, including student teaching, and become certified to teach music in the public schools. As the one-sided conversation continued, he related to me that someone at the university had contacted him about hiring a bass teacher. He recommended me, and thus, I could teach string bass on a part-time basis while working toward my degree.

I received an assistantship with a stipend and full tuition. I taught and attended school at Ohio University for one academic year, including the two adjacent summer sessions. During that time, I performed in string chamber ensembles and also played bass rather steadily on weekends with a small group in a quaint roadhouse in West Virginia, always protecting myself from the haze of tobacco smoke and occasionally my bass from flying objects when the patrons became rowdy. David Hostetler, the renowned woodcarver who was then a professor of art at Ohio University, played drums. I completed all of my university classes and laboratory requirements, wrote a thesis, and graduated with a second master's degree in 1955, this one granted by the college of education. Almost fifty years later, on September 30, 2004, I received the Ohio University fine arts distinguished alumni award.

My most significant experience at Ohio University was meeting Neal Glenn, the director of music education who introduced me to influential books pertaining to music education, particularly those written by Carl E. Seashore and James L. Mursell. I became infatuated with the psychology of music, and I had fleeting thoughts that such a discipline might offer me future academic direction. However, I did nothing about it at the time because upon graduation I went directly to Toledo to teach music in two public schools.

When I interviewed for the Toledo position, I was told I would be the director of an orchestra in one of the better high schools. After moving and settling in, I found I was assigned to two vocational high schools, one for boys and the other for girls. I was to direct a marching band and a chorus in the boys' school and to teach beginning instrumental groups in the girls' school. Not knowing my rights, but knowing the nature of my position was not written into the contract and being intimidated by the director of music education, I grimly agreed to fulfill my obligations. Without my Army band experience in the 302nd, I don't know what I would have done. Fortunately there was a student in the group, a respected and knowledgeable drum major, who helped immeasurably. The most pleasant part of my residence in Toledo was playing principal bass in the Toledo Symphony; Joseph Hawthorne was the conductor. It wasn't the world's greatest orchestra, but it provided an opportunity to become familiar with orchestral literature that had heretofore been unknown to me. Also, I became good friends with Jack Heller, concertmaster of the orchestra. In time he would follow me to Iowa and become my doctoral student in music education.

Needless to say, I was not enamored with public school teaching. Given my paucity of experience and understanding, the problems seemed enormous and insurmountable. I knew there was much for me to learn, both politically and professionally. Phil knew nothing of my plight, as we were not keeping in touch on a regular basis, but I needed advice. I wondered about returning to Eastman and getting a DMA (doctor of musical arts) in performance so I would have the necessary credentials to teach bass at a college or university. That option seemed more palatable to me than being a member of a minor symphony orchestra or traveling around the country playing a style of jazz that was out of favor with the current trend.

Then it happened. Neal Glenn called and asked if I would consider a fellowship at the University of Iowa in Iowa City. He had left Ohio University at the same time I did to become head of music education at that larger and more prestigious university. All my tuition would be paid and I would receive a special fellowship that provided $3,600 each academic year for three years. Furthermore, I would have no teaching duties. All I was required to do was attend classes, and in time, make the University of Iowa proud by gaining notoriety for the institution and me. Succinctly, I could write my own course of study with Neal as my adviser. I accepted the offer, and I left public school music teaching after one year, arriving in Iowa City just in time to register for summer school in 1956. Little did I know I would be spending sixteen eventful years of my life there. Consistent with a typical life pattern, the contrasts between the high and low events in my life were immense. Looking back, I doubt I could go through the worst parts again and survive, but I certainly would enjoy reliving the gratifying times.

III
Delight and Disillusion
(1956-1972)

Iowa summers have a reputation for being hot, but the humidity I experienced when I arrived there in June 1956 was something I had never encountered. I wondered how Native Americans had been able to stand it. The apartment I rented for my wife and me was on the second floor of a private home, and we didn't have air conditioning. I remember studying and occasionally spelling myself by gazing at the stars on a clear night before falling asleep.

One of the first things I did upon my arrival in Iowa City was to read the graduate school catalogue. I quickly ascertained I had to satisfy at least two of three requirements before I could gain admittance to the PhD program. I had to pass a minimum of two courses in statistics, a French course, and a German course (or an approved substitute language relevant to a dissertation topic).

Without asking anyone's advice, I enrolled in the obligatory two language courses and an introductory statistics course. What a summer. With great determination and travail, I managed to do satisfactory work in all three. The French examination consisted of a multiple-choice test. For the other language examination, I had to translate verbally into English a professional music or psychology journal written in German. I never spoke the languages, only read them. As a result, I am hampered when I lecture abroad because I learned to read phonetically, but never learned the proper use of accents. My attempts at speaking German proved most embarrassing when using *begábung* and receiving uproarious laughter from a German audience. I pronounced it *bégabung*, putting the accent on the first syllable instead of the second. I continue to listen to German and French, but never attempt to speak any language other than English. To this day, I am not always certain of what is being said. Remembering how my father and his business partner spoke in Yiddish is often helpful in understanding German.

It was not until the fall semester I enrolled in courses more to my liking. Although I was required to play in the university orchestra, it was not necessary to enroll in academic music courses. Most of what was being offered at Iowa I had already taken at Eastman. Also, when the required history courses were offered, a former Eastman student who was just shy of having earned his doctorate taught them. I surely wanted nothing more to do with anything that might resemble or even make reference to the Gleason outlines, those infamous historic documents that had to be memorized at Eastman word-by-word and date-by-date. I had had enough of *Orfeo – 1607*, and the like.

I began my work in the college of education, taking the second course in statistics. The dean allowed me to enroll even though I barely earned a C in the first course; as one professor wryly said, "What more can you expect of a musician." (Maybe he knew my captain in basic training at Fort Leonard Wood.) I was beginning to develop a complex about being labeled a "dumb musician." I can't remember with certainty the other courses I registered for, but they were primarily in testing, measurement, and experimental psychology. Later on, I was encouraged to elect as many courses as I pleased outside the school of music and the college of education. I did so, always choosing courses on the basis of the professors' reputations. I discovered it didn't really matter

III: Delight and Disillusion (1956-1972)

what was being taught as long as I could interact intellectually with a brilliant professor. Such professors can be found in most universities, whether in the disciplines of philosophy, religion, drama, literature, and so on, as well as in education and music. I found it valuable to take time to identify them.

For the first year, I explored courses that might point me to an as yet unidentified scholarly and academic career. I also began observing young children at play in the child welfare research station, and because of my limited public school experience I requested I be allowed to teach in the university elementary and secondary laboratory schools. My request was approved. As a matter of fact, I continued to teach vocal and instrumental classes from kindergarten through high school until the year the school closed, one year before I resigned my professorial post at the university in 1972.

My first encounter with Albert Hieronymus, whenever it was, presaged the quality of the remainder of my graduate work. More important, after many years of searching and floundering, I finally identified and embraced a lifelong vocation that motivated me and captured my passion and full attention: the psychology of music in all of its broad ramifications. Words cannot adequately express the impact Al had on my life. First it was Hal, then Sid, next Gene followed by Phil, and now Al. I wondered how I could be so fortunate. Is there a force at work unknown to the human mind? If so, why was I of all persons chosen? The reasons pale in comparison to the belief that such a sequence of events could actually take place. With great fortune I was in the right place at the right time with the right person.

Al was a professor of education and psychology who played honky-tonk piano. More impressively, he was a major author of the nationally acclaimed *Iowa Tests of Basic Skills*. As an undergraduate, Al minored in music, but for all intents and purposes, he retained little knowledge of music theory. He could hold his own when reading notation, but he was not comfortable doing so. He mostly played by ear. One day, at the conclusion of class, he said, "I hear you play bass." I affirmed his statement, and when he asked if I wanted to play sometime, again I answered, "yes." That weekend my wife and I were invited to his home, and he and I played together for a few hours. Being unaware of my professional background and referring to me as "one of those academic musicians," he was astonished I knew the changes to tunes familiar to him and could "keep a beat." We became fast friends and played together numerous times. Whenever possible, I took the opportunity to ask questions about the psychology of music and related issues of measurement and evaluation. He was a doctoral student at Iowa when Carl Seashore was dean of the graduate school. Though Al never took a class from him, he often made a point of being available to walk home from the university with the dean, hoping it might offer the opportunity to pose relevant academic questions.

A few months later, a column in the city newspaper recounted an interview with a physician who recently was appointed to a professorship in the university medical school. His complaint was he enjoyed playing jazz as an avocation, but there was no one in town for him to play with. When the article was brought to my attention, I recognized the doctor's name, Kenneth Hubel. Kenn is an alto sax player. I had played with him in Stamford, Greenwich, and Darien, Connecticut and Rye, New York when we were in high school, and then later in Rochester, New York, while I was attending Eastman and he was a student in the medical school of the University of Rochester. Before long, he joined Al and me, and we had a trio. Then medical student Patrick Plunkett, who was boarding at Kenn's home and played tenor sax, joined the group. Finally, we discovered a drummer in computer specialist John Stanley. Thus, we had an ensemble that played for our own enjoyment at least once a week, rotating events at one another's home. Soon, friends, both students

III: Delight and Disillusion (1956-1972)

and faculty, were invited to listen to us or to sit in, whichever they pleased. I loved every minute of it.

One time when the group was asked to play for a benefit at a church in town, a fellow walked up with a trombone in hand and asked if he could sit in. We asked him what he wanted to play, and he answered, "Whatever you guys want." Someone called a tune, and his chorus was unbelievable. He turned out to be one of the greatest Dixieland trombonists I ever heard. We soon learned that he, George Patterson, was a Methodist minister and a self-taught musician. He became a member of the group, sometimes playing flute and guitar. Then, a dentist who had played clarinet with Charlie Spivak, named Al Soucek, joined the group. The camaraderie was wonderful; we all enjoyed one another's musicianship and personalities. I was the only one in the group who had studied at a music conservatory.

As a student, I learned a great deal about measurement and psychology from Al, mostly on an informal basis. I would read something and later initiate a discussion about it with him whenever the opportunity presented itself. Other times I would find Al weeding somewhere on his farm, sit down beside him, and ask him to comment, for example, on the differences between a norms-referenced test and a criterion-referenced test. The quality and length of the answer exceeded what I might have expected if I had raised the subject in class.

Al stopped in the hall one day when I was talking to one of his colleagues and inquired whether I was familiar with the *Drake Musical Aptitude Tests*. The battery was relatively new, and I knew nothing about it. He gave me his desk-reference LP record along with an accompanying test manual and suggested I review it and give him my appraisal. I did. That discussion was particularly important, because it led to my initial interest in the nature, source, description, and measurement of music aptitudes and later influenced my identification of a dissertation topic. Subsequently,

Al asked if I had ever considered writing my own music aptitude test. He knew the *Seashore Measures of Musical Talents*, originally published in 1919 and revised in 1939, was a great pioneering effort, but they left something to be desired in terms of experimental validity. He thought with my musical background and knowledge about and interest in measurement and psychology, I might make a worthwhile contribution to the profession. Given the expanded and powerful modern statistical techniques at my disposal, I could create an up-to-date music aptitude test battery. His suggestion and encouragement ultimately led to the development of my first, and perhaps one of my most scholarly endeavors, the *Musical Aptitude Profile*, known by the acronym MAP. Largely based on Al's recommendation, the Houghton Mifflin Company published the first edition in 1965 after eight years of developmental research.

By late 1957, I had completed all of my coursework but had yet to finish my dissertation. I was able to move through the program quickly because I had attended all summer school sessions. Also, largely due to the intervention of Himie Voxman, head of the school of music, I was permitted to take my oral and written comprehensive examinations in music even though his course was the only one I had taken in the school of music. However, as noted, throughout my student days I had been required to play bass in the university orchestra. I wrote for several days on music theory, history, and literature; music education; educational research; educational psychology; measurement; and statistics. I did well enough that my comprehensive orals were waived, though I had to take the traditional orals in defense of my doctoral research. I was then allowed to move immediately to writing my dissertation. Al and I had talked so much about the topic that I was able to write a proposal quickly and have it approved by an eclectic academic committee. Because of the interdisciplinary nature of the research problem, the validity of the Drake tests, the faculty suggested I have co-advisers. Neal Glenn in music

III: Delight and Disillusion (1956-1972)

education and Leonard Feldt in educational tests and measurement consented to serve in those roles. I conducted the research in cooperation with students attending the university laboratory schools and shortly thereafter I documented and defended what I wrote. I graduated with a PhD in June 1958.

Immediately upon graduation, I was hired as an assistant professor of music education by the University of Iowa and began teaching undergraduate and graduate courses that summer. Also, I was assigned several doctoral students and assumed the responsibility of directing their PhD dissertations. My teaching assignments were divided between the college of education and the school of music, but the theses and dissertations I directed were only those of students enrolled in the school of music.

A significant series of events began in 1957 when my oldest daughter, Jaimeson Beth, was born. She was followed by Pamela Anne in 1959 and Alison Carrie in 1962. My wife had made it known she would like to have children. I suspect she was growing weary of being alone so much of the time. Of course, I was very busy studying and completing the requirements for my doctorate. I would leave the apartment at about 6:30 am, usually before my wife had awakened, and ride my bike to school. Generally I would return home long after the dinner hour. I obliged her wish to have children, and it goes without saying that my daughters have brought me much joy, especially because they are such fine persons. However, I also feel sorrow because I left the children in 1969 when they were young when my wife and I separated and then divorced in 1970. I no longer dread anything more that life might have to offer, because nothing could be worse than having been forced to leave the house very early one morning while the children were still asleep, never to live with them again on a permanent basis. Unequivocally, it was the most difficult and painful day of my life.

As colleagues, Al and I remained as close as when we were professor and student. With his assistance, I completed the initial design of the *Gordon Measures of Musical Aptitude*, the precursor of the *Musical Aptitude Profile*, in fall 1958. I had already undertaken much of the preliminary work because I had written the introduction and related research sections of my dissertation in more detail than necessary.

I labored for nearly eight years, researching and designing the *Musical Aptitude Profile*. Most of that time was spent in close association with Al. We met several days each week for hours at a time. We scrutinized every detail of my proposals for various research studies to validate MAP and construct the many subtests included in the initial research. I not only learned how to better express myself through the written word, but also how to professionally engage in measurement investigations. Simply stated, at the feet of Al I had more than a decade of post-doctoral education. Without his guidance and influence, MAP would probably never have been created or published. I also garnered much ancillary knowledge at the time from Leonard Feldt, who graciously acted as a statistical co-adviser on many of the doctoral dissertations I directed.

I feel it is important to mention, as I look back on the design and content of MAP, that I believe a power within me was guiding my work. In a sense, the energy worked through me. With so little knowledge and experience, how could I have known what to ask in the test battery and how to ask it? That undertaking was far beyond my understanding at the time, and even now I continue to learn from what I did then.

This concurrence revitalized my interest in mysticism, and I have not lost the zeal accompanying that kind of power. Perhaps that is why I am such an ardent follower of Joseph Campbell and his work, much of which is based on the writings of Carl G. Jung and Jung's ideas about the collective unconscious. As they assert, dreams are the myths of individuals, and myths are the dreams of humankind.

Al enjoyed arguing with me about every detail, musical and otherwise, especially the psychological constructs of each subtest to be included in the test battery. He would sit at one desk, and I would sit at another facing him in his office. At times, our professional arguments became so loud that colleagues would pop their heads in the doorway to be assured no physical violence was taking place. Once he threw a book at me; I ducked, and it broke the glass in a bookcase behind me, but the argument continued. Both of us stood our ground, and when the next meeting took place, we began as if the previous meeting was something we might have imagined. I am not sure I ever changed his mind about anything, but he certainly made me think deeply about my own convictions.

Some aspects of my teaching at Iowa bear only indirectly on my professional development, but they are worth relating. When my appointment at Iowa became public, I was summoned to the office of one of my former professors. He said he was in a hurry, but he would like to offer me some free advice and I could "take it or leave it." I was to remember the following: 1) one good book is worth a hundred journal articles; 2) don't try to change the personality of the university, because soon after you leave, whatever you might have managed to change will revert right back to what it was before you arrived; and 3) you should teach to the upper five percent of students, because the others are not worth your time. I almost immediately agreed with the first two points. I understood how the third point might apply to university students, but not how it would apply to students in lower grades. I have always maintained that individual differences among younger students must be taken into consideration in the instructional process. As he was walking out the door, he turned and uttered, "Remember, your students come first, you come second, and the university comes last. Avoid committee work as much as possible."

During the summer I taught very early in the morning; my first class began at 7:00 am. The intense heat later in the day and the lack of air conditioning and fans necessitated the early hour. Nonetheless, I was expected to wear a tie when I taught, though a long-sleeved shirt or jacket was not required. I maintain the tie habit to this day, feeling a bit naked if I do not wear one when teaching. My classroom was next to a speech pathology laboratory. I must have had a reputation as being a cooperative guy, because when my class ended, a student who stuttered and needed speech therapy would be waiting outside my door. As I was leaving, he or she would begin speaking to me. I was informed in advance to listen patiently and not help with any word the student was attempting to pronounce. Because I frequently consumed a large amount of coffee to enable myself to be alert to teach so early in the day, one can imagine my distress as I stood against the wall impatiently waiting for these students to conclude a sentence or conversation. My contributions in this matter were greatly appreciated by my colleagues. One student explained to me that although he stuttered when speaking he never stuttered when singing. I have since learned that is common but wonder if anyone has ever discovered why it is so. The reason might have implications for research in the psychology of music.

As coauthor of the *Iowa Tests of Basic Skills*, Al was friendly with the officers in the Houghton Mifflin Company, the publisher of ITBS. Often when executives and salespersons were in town they attended parties at Al's home, and our musical ensemble performed. A grand time was always had by all. On one occasion in 1962, Hal Miller, director of the test division of Houghton Mifflin, attended the party and asked me to take a walk with him. He told me Al had apprised him of my work in developing a music aptitude test, and he was impressed with the results of the prepublication validity studies. After determining I had not signed a contract with another publisher who had shown some interest in the test battery (Carl

III: Delight and Disillusion (1956-1972)

Seashore's son Harold, who was director of the test division of the Psychological Corporation), he asked if I might like to publish the test with his company when it was completed. It did not take long to say "yes," and we shook hands to seal the agreement. I received a contract a week or so later. What an opportunity! I was only an assistant professor with no professional reputation outside Iowa City. Most persons would have made substantial sacrifices to achieve such status. It was the making of my career, and of course it was all Al's doing. The offer was a great boost for me personally as well, because I know Al would never have taken the trouble if he did not respect the meticulous work the measurement tool represented.

Little did I know what the future held. The nationwide standardization program of the test battery had to be outlined and overseen, and once that project was completed, an extensive test manual had to be written. The editors in the publishing house concluded from a prepublication survey that the majority of music teachers were uninformed about the nature of music aptitude and its distinction from music achievement. Thus, the test manual would have to contain an extensive section on the interpretation and use of scores garnered from each of the seven subtests. I would not have been able to accomplish at least the first two of those endeavors without Al's assistance. Thus, our weekly meetings and predictable noisy and contentious debates went on for at least another three years until the test battery was published, usually to the dismay of our colleagues who had offices nearby. All of the answer sheets from the standardization program, in excess of 10,000, were machine scored. The computer specialist delivered mounds of data to me to be transformed and analyzed every day. To satisfy Al, I had to replicate much of what the computer had already accomplished using a desk calculator. In that way, he knew I would learn "what it is all about." To this day, I am compelled to review completed answer sheets in my research projects even though computers eliminate the need for this time-consuming chore.

All the time MAP was being developed I was carrying a full load of undergraduate and graduate teaching. Moreover, I taught students in the university's elementary and secondary laboratory schools, made systematic observations of children attending the university preschool, and consulted with the preschool faculty.

As the content and design of MAP was being experimented with, the method of establishing validity for the test battery was a constant source of conversation between Al and me. In 1963 we decided concurrent (or criterion-related) validity, although a necessary preliminary step in the validation process, would not be sufficient. Only the state of the art would be acceptable and that was the completion of a longitudinal predictive validity study. The problem with concurrent validity for an aptitude test is, given a correlation coefficient, only the relation between factors can be explained, not the causation of the relation. To solve the problem, an investigation had to be designed in the following manner: the aptitude test must be administered before any instruction takes place. Then students are given instruction over a period of years. Finally, the accomplishment of the students is measured and those post-instruction achievement scores are correlated with the pre-instruction aptitude scores. Whatever the magnitude of the correlation coefficient, the cause of the relation is obvious: the degree of potential must be responsible for level of achievement. However, realistically to undertake and complete a longitudinal predictive validity study is expensive both in time and money. Being the first person to accomplish the uniquely designed task and to report the results for a music test in an extensive and professional manner, I gained recognition from influential persons in allied disciplines. I have conducted similar studies for all my music aptitude tests following this first one, and to this day I know of no other person who has undertaken corresponding research in music test development.

III: Delight and Disillusion (1956-1972)

The study was made possible by James Neilson and the National Association of Instrument Manufacturers, which granted me 250 new brass and woodwind instruments. I then lent the instruments to fourth and fifth grade students in several schools in Iowa and Wisconsin at no cost with the understanding that every student in a given classroom who was continuously enrolled in the school would have to study the instrument for three years and attend at least one group instrumental music class or private lesson each week. Additional study was not restricted. The University of Iowa cooperated by providing a sizable grant to print answer sheets, rent computer time to score the answer sheets and analyze data, to travel, and so on. Before and after the end of each of three years of instruction, MAP was readministered, and achievement criteria were gathered for every student. The resultant validity coefficients after three years were impressive (as high as .75 for the composite score), and all subtest scores were found impervious to the effects of practice and training. The University of Iowa published the complete study in monograph form in 1967, as Volume V in *Studies in the Psychology of Music*. Carl Seashore initiated the series and edited the first four volumes. Following the publications of MAP and the monograph, I was promoted to associate professor, and shortly after, in 1967, to full professor. In 1968, my title changed to professor of music and education, but my responsibilities remained the same.

Much to my astonishment, and though I hesitate to admit my naiveté, my interest in music aptitude was not acceptable to all educators, music and otherwise. This censure was not simply a result of not understanding the difference between music aptitude and music achievement. There were political and philosophical problems as well. Some educators suggested I was trying to exclude "untalented" students from participating in school music activities, and, worse yet, my undeclared purpose was to label students permanently as "unmusical." Nothing could have been further from the truth. My primary intent was to contribute to the quality of music instruction for all students by giving teachers objective information that would assist them in teaching to the individual musical needs of all of their students. I was attempting to provide teachers with objective measures so they could make substantial subjective evaluations and adapt instruction in various dimensions of music aptitude to the musical differences among students, from the very lowest to the very highest scoring in the class. Some educators or critics did not comprehend that the most important purpose of any test is not to give grades or to make students vain or insecure, but rather, to improve instruction by being certain every student successfully and fully achieves at the level of his or her potential. As a result, students with high music aptitude do not become bored, and students with low music aptitude do not become frustrated with school music. The majority of students may even learn to like school music as much as they like the popular music of their generation. This criticism was not my first introduction to reality, but it was potent. Because I was in the forefront, I had to face the assembly alone. I was hurt, if not offended, that my offer of help was not being graciously accepted, and I was compelled to deal with a cadre of adversaries.

Some faultfinders went so far as to call me racist or a Nazi. They reminded me that the founding fathers of our country wrote that all men are created equal. I commented to them that any thinking person would have to acknowledge all individuals should have equal rights under the law, but all individuals are not equally talented. Certainly, there was no equal to Mozart or Einstein in the group I was addressing. Nonetheless, they refused to concede that the Preamble to the Constitution was written in poetic style. I finally concluded my detractors were actually fearful of two things: 1) knowing the level of their own music aptitude and 2) knowing the music aptitude levels of their students (because they were unaware of how to use the information to improve instruction). It was not unusual for a teacher to ask if he or she should cease teaching because of an obtained low music aptitude score, or for a teacher to ask if it were really possible to adapt instruction to students' individual musical differences. Although they, as teachers, probably knew more about the history and theory of music than any student in their classroom, it was difficult for them to accept the fact they might have average music aptitude. That is not atypical; on average, approximately one-third of students in every class and ensemble have higher music aptitudes than their music teacher.

My undergraduate teaching responsibilities included two sections of an elective course: Music for the Classroom Teacher. Given the research data and broader teaching experience I acquired in the previous decade, I decided to write a book for classroom teachers and be my own publisher and distributor. I titled the paperback book *How We Learn When We Learn Music*. Somehow, Charles Leonhard, who was editing a series of music education textbooks for Prentice-Hall, discovered the second edition and contacted me in 1969. He asked if I would like to incorporate the content of the book into a new book to be included in this series. I agreed, and after considerable reading in allied disciplines, *The Psychology of Music Teaching* was published in 1971. To the best of my knowledge, it was the first book in music education to colligate general principles of learning and to organize and combine them into a Music Learning Theory.

Most concepts pertaining to Music Learning Theory were derived indirectly from my research in music aptitude. During its development and upon publication of the *Musical Aptitude Profile*, I erroneously expected that teachers would understand how to make reasonable use of music aptitude test results. However, it soon became obvious they were not. Sequential learning in music instruction was given almost no consideration in the college and university preparation of music teachers. Also, most music teachers were bereft of methods to teach to students' individual musical differences. Thus, I culled what I could from writings of educational psychologists about general principles of learning and adapted them to music education. Being aware that most of what I wrote in *The Psychology of Music Teaching* was theoretical, the urgent need for relevant empirical research was compelling. It was then that my absorption in Music Learning Theory and music aptitude had for all intents and purposes removed me from quotidian life. The sum and substance of the subject matter not only overwhelmed me, it consumed me.

The topic was just as exciting then as it is now. However, its presentation to the music education community was at least fifty years ahead of its time. Even today, more than thirty years later, I believe myriad music teachers may still be uncomfortable with Music Learning Theory. To accept its concepts requires time and change, and most teachers and humans in general do not embrace change easily. Specifically, to shift the emphasis in music education from promoting the teaching process to understanding the learning process requires courage and risk. Good methodology must be based on principles of learning. I believe the foremost egregious problem in current music education practice is most teachers teach the way they were taught and not in accord with the way students learn. Unfortunately, many think teaching and learning are synonymous.

To identify with Music Learning Theory presupposes a lifelong commitment to research in learning and its application to teaching. Nothing is static; quality methodology in teaching is no exception, especially when pursued in conjunction with Music Learning Theory. To that end, Music Learning Theory has taken on a life of its own. Without changing its basic tenets, many musicians and educators have adapted Music Learning Theory to their own teaching styles and personalities.

Stepping back for a moment, I should explain the *Iowa Tests of Music Literacy* (ITML) battery was published in 1970. Much of the test battery's content was already put together to serve as part of validity criteria in the three-year longitudinal predictive validity study of the *Musical Aptitude Profile*. All that remained was to direct the standardization program and to write the test manual. I undertook both of those tasks without Al's assistance. The Bureau of Educational Research and Service of the College of Education at the University of Iowa asked to publish ITML, and I agreed without giving either of my two publishers at the time an opportunity to review it. Although it has by no means gained wide acceptance within the music education profession, I am very proud of ITML because I believe it was the first, and still is, the only music achievement test to comprise different levels of content difficulty while still measuring parallel skills from the first to the sixth level. As I explain in the test manual, a single-level achievement test, as compared to a multilevel achievement test, suffers in reliability and therefore, in validity. If the same test is used as a pre-test as well as a post-test, some of the questions will be too difficult at the beginning of instruction and too easy at the conclusion of instruction. Thus, valid academic achievement tests include separate tests for students of different ages.

The *Iowa Tests of Music Literacy* was revised in 1991, and at that time, the copyright was transferred to GIA. The revision of any type of achievement test requires the establishment of new norms. In the more than twenty years between the 1968 and 1991 standardization programs, the norms remained constant, much to my dismay. The only conclusion is not much is taking place in music education. Students' skills in audiating, reading, and notating music in various tonalities and meters have remained dormant for all intents and purposes. Trying to establish responsibility for such an unconscionable state of affairs would be useless, but both schools and families should take note of this intolerable situation and attempt to ameliorate it. The Gordon Institute for Music Learning (GIML) published a monograph I authored in which I reported the data and outlined the deplorable situation, but it has gone unnoticed by the music education power structure and political bureaucracy. Perhaps because of embarrassment or fear of public reaction, the music education hierarchy refuses to acknowledge the compelling facts, and as a result, responsible officials are at a loss to know what to do about the situation.

I must learn to accept the fact that my work will probably not influence or be accepted by the mainstream of current music educators. Integrity and intelligence as well as musicianship are requisite. I am content knowing at least my ideas may assist in retaining capable persons in the music education profession and attracting those with open and motivated minds who have not yet developed fear of change.

I cannot help but be reminded that even intelligent and musical persons refuse to change their opinions, regardless of facts. I remember as a graduate student at Iowa, I completed a small research project in the university laboratory schools in which I compared the value of beginning group instrumental music instruction to private lessons. The results were patently obvious. Students who were given group lessons developed better intonation, rhythm, tone quality, and overall musicianship than those who were given private instruction, though those given private instruction were more advanced in instrumental technique. When I reported my results to the academic community, professors in the school of music summoned and scolded me for spreading such outrageous and unwarranted notions. I showed them the research results, but they wanted none of it. After all, they had developed a reputation for giving private lessons, and for editing and publishing volumes of literature advocating private study that were being sold widely. I was depicted as an inexperienced young upstart who had to be put in his place, and no music professor would publicly or privately defend my research on this topic.

My mother, Carrie,
April 14, 1918.

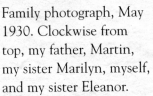

Me at 8 months,
May 1928.

Family photograph, May 1930. Clockwise from top, my father, Martin, my sister Marilyn, myself, and my sister Eleanor.

Me at 3 1/2 years old,
March 21, 1931.

With Rex, 1944.

1946, as a member of the 302nd Army Band.

March 1947. A night at the Officers' Club during intermission with Lester, Jacobs, and Ramsey—all great men.

EASTMAN SCHOOL OF MUSIC
Of The University of Rochester

Kilbourn Hall

SIXTH GRADUATION RECITAL

585th in the Series of Graduation Recitals

EDWIN GORDON, *Double Bass*
CLINE OTEY, *Violin*

(Candidates for the Degree Master of Music in Music Literature)
Students of Oscar Zimmerman and André de Ribaupierre

Program

Concerto for Double Bass   DRAGONETTI
    Allegro moderato
    Andante
    Allegro giusto
        Mr. Gordon
            Alice Seitz *at the piano*

Three Pieces by Corelli for Violin and Bass   Arr. by ANTON TORELLO
    Largo
    Sarabande
    Gavotte
        Mr. Otey and Mr. Gordon

Sonata for Piano and Violin, Opus 47 (Kreutzer)   BEETHOVEN
    Adagio sostenuto
    Andante con variazioni
    Finale: Presto
        Mr. Otey
            Thelma Johanos *at the piano*

At 12:10 o'clock, Wednesday
November 26, 1952

1952, Eastman School of Music recital program and official graduation photo.

1953, Philip Sklar—outstanding bass teacher. I studied with him in New York City.

1968, my daughters, left to right, Pam, Carrie, Jaime.

1965, Albert Hieronymus.

1971, The house I built following my divorce, Lake McBride, Iowa.

Maria Runfola, Buffalo State University of New York. A great assistant in music education 1972–1979.

August 18, 1976, my wedding day with Carol.

1977, my daughters, (left to right) Carrie, Pam, Jaime.

1981, playing bass in our Marion Station home.

1986, Sugarloaf.

1991, teaching tonal patterns at Weber State College, Ogden, Utah.

1994, Lake Elsinore, California. Lunch with three truly great people, my wife, Carol, and Mae and Sid Weiss.

October 1998, lunch with their dad, (left to right) Carrie, Pam, and Jaime.

1998 with Carol and the programmer Robert Moog designed for my testing in 1974.

July 1999. Teaching very young children at the University of New Mexico, Albuquerque.

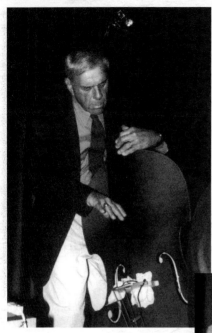

September 15, 2000.
Playing bass in Lisbon.

2004. Gordon Instiute for
Music Learning Theory
of Korea.

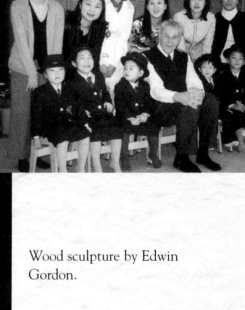

Wood sculpture by Edwin
Gordon.

III: Delight and Disillusion (1956-1972)

Significant events of a positive nature occurred during my tenure at Iowa. I became general editor of Volumes V through X of the *Studies in the Psychology of Music*. (For purposes of copyright law, the title of these six volumes had to be changed to *Experimental Research in the Psychology of Music: Studies in the Psychology of Music*.) Being responsible for the series boasting an illustrious group of advocate editors was quite an honor because, as I have explained, Carl Seashore initiated the series and over the years the journals have enjoyed a covetous reputation. Many of the articles are still referenced, and others serve as models and as standards for papers that appear in allied professional journals. When I left Iowa, the publication of the series ceased and has not been reactivated. This is an unfortunate symptom of the times because every research report was published in full in the series. Important tables were not eliminated, and texts were not abridged for the sake of brevity, as is so often the case in contemporary academic journals. Moreover, I did not reject papers simply because tests of probability did not yield statistically significant results. In my professional view, respectable research that included null hypotheses that had to be retained as well as those that were rejected needed to be published. After all, knowing a researched topic was not found worthy of pursuing is just as important as knowing a hypothesis might prove to have merit. Who can deny ongoing worthy research is valuable knowledge for a reader? To that extent, the series paralleled today's monograph series published by GIA and the Gordon Institute for Music Learning in which an entire volume may be devoted exclusively to one or two research reports.

Another event may seem of lesser importance, but as I engage in reflection, I think it was of consequence. Because the primary pursuit of the educational division of the Houghton Mifflin Company was to sell textbooks, and not necessarily tests, let alone music tests, the salesmen were largely uninformed about the value of the *Musical Aptitude Profile*. They worked on commission, and their time was precious. They needed to talk to school administrators about products that would apply to all students, products that would sustain continued sales. Because MAP is a test of stabilized music aptitude, it needs to be administered only once to students. Although students' scores usually increase with chronological age, their relative standing in a class, their percentile rank, remains relatively stable. Obviously, a salesman's commission for selling a textbook for each student or a test battery that has different levels and thus, is continuously administered year after year, is considerably more than for selling a test that needs to be administered only once throughout a student's school career.

Therefore, it was no surprise when I was asked to speak to sales personnel at annual company meetings in an effort to persuade them it was important to take the time to familiarize school administrators, counselors, and teachers with the purposes of MAP. That was no easy task. Because it was so arduous, I learned a great deal about how to address large and critical audiences. I would not be experiencing much success today as a speaker were it not for those early encounters. I must have done reasonably well because MAP was rarely advertised by the company. Thus I believe its acceptance was largely due to the enthusiasm of the salesmen and their knowledge about the measurement and importance of music aptitude, which they absorbed from my lectures. One of the salesmen, Robert Janis, who was particularly committed to MAP and befriended me throughout the years, later became president of the test division of the company when it was renamed the Riverside Press.

Before concluding my retrospection of my experiences at the University of Iowa and Iowa City, an important fact must be explained. As already alluded to, I received a sizable grant from the University of Iowa and hundreds of music instruments from

III: Delight and Disillusion (1956-1972)

the National Association of Band Manufacturers to conduct the three-year longitudinal predictive validity study of MAP. Consequently, I felt uneasy about accepting royalties from the Houghton Mifflin Company solely for myself. True, I did the work, but in addition to all of Al Hieronymus's efforts, I used funds other than my own to pursue the research. It seemed only fair that the royalties should be divided in an equitable manner. The issue was resolved to my satisfaction when the University of Iowa became a coauthor of the test and half of the royalties were deposited in a non-taxable research fund that would support my future research. The idea worked well. Over the years, I was able to use that money to conduct additional longitudinal validity studies and related research in music aptitude and music achievement and to fund the research efforts and ancillary needs of some of my graduate students. Largely in appreciation for my establishment of international norms for the test and consulting with teachers and administrators who were using MAP in their schools, I received a modest check each year from the publisher.

Not until I was divorced did a problem arise. After I made the legally agreed upon child support and alimony payments, I had very little money remaining at the end of the month to sustain my basic needs of food, housing, and clothing. Iowa, not unlike other universities, had a reputation for employing recent graduates who held promise and would be so honored by the opportunity to hold a professorship at the institution they would accept incommensurate compensation. Consequently, I officially requested a modest raise in salary to ameliorate my situation, indicating I did not want to leave the University of Iowa for the purpose of simply increasing my salary. Nonetheless, my request was rejected. Perhaps administrators took the position they were not responsible for my domestic problems, and thus I should seek assistance elsewhere. There was also the possibility my receiving monetary assistance was refused because I had turned down an offer to be of head of music education after Neal Glenn left to join the faculty at the University of Miami, which would have brought me an increase in salary. I did not want to be tied down by administrative duties and thus prevented from doing research. With the closing of the laboratory schools for fiscal reasons, the official responsibilities as head of music education would have been enormous.

Because administrators knew I was aware my departure would require a review of the legality for me to continue to secure funds to support my ongoing and future research, I believe they could not envision I would leave the university. Moreover, even though my salary was relatively low, I enjoyed my work and my professional associations with able colleagues so much, it seemed inconceivable to them I would sever those relationships. When I signed the MAP three-way contract with the publisher and the university, I never thought an unforeseen adverse condition could force me to leave Iowa at some later date. Thus, no provision was made in the contract for that possibility. Nonetheless, the unanticipated event occurred, and my need to apply for a position at another university to earn sufficient money to live even modestly became a reality.

When it became clear I would need to find outside sources to supplement my income, I decided to let it be known nationally that my services were available and I would leave Iowa under the appropriate conditions. Within a few weeks I was offered a position at the State University of New York at Buffalo with a much higher salary than I was earning at Iowa. After several visits, I accepted the position of professor of music. My only concern was leaving my three young daughters behind in an environment less than wholesome. University officials informed me I would no longer have access to my research fund. However, Iowa begrudgingly allocated a moderate sum to allow me to complete a research project in Buffalo I had initiated before I left Iowa; this was the last funding I received from the university's

III: Delight and Disillusion (1956-1972)

portion of MAP royalties until the copyright was obtained by GIA almost thirty years later. Given that information, the events surrounding my divorce should be clearer. The memories still remain disturbing.

I have continually made reference to the unhappiness surrounding my first marriage. In 1968 I discovered my wife was seeing another man who was considerably older than either of us and who was a close professional colleague of mine. He attended our jazz parties with his wife. In spite of having the children my wife had said would fulfill her needs, she was nevertheless unhappy. I continued to spend little time with her and devoted most of my free time to the girls. Evidently she was lonely, vengeful, or both. Whether or not her affair was an attempt to get my attention, I will never know. Moreover, I cannot be certain, but I believe her companion was an alcoholic. Soon the two of them were meeting secretly (I was perhaps the last person in Iowa City to learn it), and she began drinking more heavily until it seemed that she too was an alcoholic. The situation reached a point where I could not reason with her, and she refused to acknowledge the abhorrent environment to which our children were being exposed. I later learned that every Saturday when she was supposedly going to the Davenport, Iowa, area to shop, she was actually meeting her male companion while I was spending time with our daughters.

We also developed a Sunday routine. He, his wife, my wife, and I would spend the afternoon and evening playing bridge or watching football games, eating and drinking. Eventually their behavior became so blatant that I had to recognize their relationship. I was more hurt by his duplicity than I was angry. One Sunday night, he refused to leave our house after his wife drove home alone. I told him to leave, but he decided not to, and my wife told me I should leave if I didn't approve of his staying or of their rowdy drinking. I did exactly that. I put whatever clothes

I could gather quickly and my bass in our car and deposited them in my university office. I then returned the car to our garage and rode my bicycle back to the university, sleeping on my desk that night and remaining there the following day and night. On Monday, I taught my regularly scheduled classes, freshening up by taking my daily shower in the boys' locker room of the university laboratory schools. I borrowed a reclining beach chair and slept on it for two weeks until I received my monthly paycheck and was able to rent a small apartment in a privately owned dormitory designed for university students.

Aside from being crushed by my former colleague's betrayal, I felt abandoned by my friends. I was later told they felt they could not afford to get involved. They reasoned that the university was too closely knit for them to take sides. No colleague offered assistance or comfort, let alone money. I needed money desperately because my wife had spent all the money in our savings account, and our checking account was overdrawn. My daughters would frequently come by my office, poorly dressed and hungry to ask for money for food and other necessities. I had little to give them. An acquaintance, a professor at another big ten university, heard of my plight and sent a hundred dollar bill by mail to me at the university. My pride was such that my initial reaction was to return it immediately, but thinking it through and realizing the financial needs of the children, I kept it and returned the loan later when my financial situation improved.

My wife had her lawyer issue a cease and desist order against me. Living in a small apartment, my nights were lonely, except when the girls would visit once a week. I think I was about to go mad in such small quarters, so quiet and empty of children's voices after my day's work was completed. I also had no idea when I returned to my erstwhile home how much it had meant to have my terrier, Tiny, bark and greet me.

III: Delight and Disillusion (1956-1972)

I would be remiss not to mention a doctoral student, Thelma Volger, without whose kindness I might not have survived the ordeal. Among other things, she allowed me to borrow her car once a week so I could drive to another city to teach an extension class and earn extra money I desperately needed. Often she would accompany me on the trip, and I was able to express my anguish to her as she was a great listener, a wise woman, and a good friend.

The divorce negotiations did not go smoothly. I wanted to sue for custody of the girls, but was advised against it by my lawyers. They told me if I could not prove my daughters' mother was unfit, meaning she was not providing food, shelter, and/or clothing with the child support money, I did not stand a chance of securing custody of them under Iowa legal statutes. Traditional Iowa law always favored the mother. Thus, I would be wasting my money and time. Moreover, my lawyers convinced me if I contested her custody of our daughters, the case probably would go to court and the unpleasant facts would become public. The ones who would suffer most would be the children rather than her and her partner. Also, I was fond of the other man's wife, who would have been stained by this situation, and none of this was any more her doing than mine.

In 1970, about a year after I left the house, the divorce was finalized. A few months after that my father died, and I was informed he had left me some money. All the time I had worked for him in the awning business, I was never paid. I accepted that as natural because everyone in our home was expected to contribute in some way to the family income. As it turned out, the money I received after my father's death was in the form of bonds my father had bought in my name with the earnings I would have received if he had paid me directly. He was wise enough to know I would desperately need money some day much more than I needed it at the time. He did not want me to have it until I understood its value.

Still not anticipating I would ever leave the University of Iowa, I used the funds to buy a lakefront lot a few miles out of Iowa City. I was then able to borrow money from a bank to build a house by the lake. I hired an architect, and to save money I became my own contractor. It took about six months to complete the small but attractive house, during which time I lived in the basement. The children visited quite often. We went on boat rides and had delightful picnics, and my mental outlook improved. Nonetheless, I was in the house only a few months before it became obvious I had to leave the university. I could no longer avoid the painful fact that I had to separate myself from the University of Iowa because I needed additional money to make the mortgage deadlines, to maintain my payments of alimony and child support, and to be able to offer the girls what they required to maintain their mental stability and satisfy their everyday needs. Occasionally they would visit me without toiletries, adequate underclothes, or other necessities, and I would purchase the needed articles for them.

After I submitted my letter of resignation and accepted a full professorship with tenure from SUNY at Buffalo, administrators at the University of Iowa asserted that they were astonished I ever seriously contemplated leaving Iowa City, and they wanted to discuss the possibility I might reconsider my planned separation. Of course, the time for that had long passed. I put the lake house up for sale, and it was sold in a few weeks. I said my goodbyes to the children, promised them they could visit me as often as they desired and that I would stay in constant touch with them by telephone. Then I was off. As I remember, I stopped to teach a weeklong seminar at the University of Wisconsin in Madison on my way to my new faculty position. During my final interview in Buffalo, I had rented an apartment in Williamsville, New York, a Buffalo suburb.

III: Delight and Disillusion (1956-1972)

Two university appointments later, while teaching at Temple University, I received a letter from the University of Iowa stating that I had been selected to receive a distinguished alumni achievement award. It was to be conferred at ceremonies in Iowa City on May 30, 1992, exactly twenty years after my departure from Iowa City. Judith Svengalis, a longtime friend and student from my Iowa days, had submitted the nomination and joined my daughters, Carol, and me along with other Iowa City friends to celebrate that happy, nostalgic occasion.

IV
Pausing and Passing Midway
(1972-1979)

I drove to Buffalo in August 1972, knowing that a large amount of organizational work had to be undertaken to begin my teaching and administrative duties in September. One reason I was being paid so well was because I agreed to be director of music education in addition to my teaching responsibilities. I can't explain why I was willing to be an administrator in Buffalo but not in Iowa. Perhaps it was the challenge of dealing with unfamiliar colleagues in new surroundings. I was expected to reconstruct the undergraduate music education curriculum and design a PhD program in music education to be granted from the department of music similar to the one at Iowa. Until that time, the department had offered only a DEd (doctor of education), and the degree was under the umbrella of the college of education.

I was certain I could accomplish all that was asked of me because one of the conditions for my acceptance of the new position was that a former doctoral student, who was teaching in the Iowa City public schools at the time, would be hired as an assistant professor and support me in my endeavors. I contributed to part of his initial salary. There was only one other full time faculty member in music education, Maria Hale, who has since resumed her maiden name,

Maria Runfola. As it turned out, she alone was all I needed to master what I had to know and how to accomplish it. She learned very quickly and adapted comfortably and eagerly to my perspective. The faculty member I brought with me became a major disappointment. However, on the positive side, I should mention that Thelma Volger, the doctoral candidate from Iowa, had not completed writing her dissertation at the time of my departure. Consequently, the dean of the graduate school at Iowa granted me permission to remain her adviser and direct the final chapters of her report in Buffalo. I was able to secure an assistantship for her at Buffalo, and she too helped me perform my obligations.

Perhaps the most persuasive reason for me to accept the position at SUNY–Buffalo was the opportunity to become familiar with the chair of the department of music, who had a keen interest in the history of music theory. Because he was well acquainted with my publications and liked my point of view and research interests, he pursued me, promising to assist in developing scholarly academic programs in music education and the psychology of music. He acknowledged the importance of music education in contributing to the integrity of a music department. During the interview process, he gave me early treatises on music theory he had translated, which I found to be highly informative. Through them, particularly Étienne Loulié's *Elements or Principles of Music*, I discovered the answers to many questions I had, particularly those pertaining to the transition of early signs to modern measure signatures during the period from 1650 to 1800. I anticipated I would exchange ideas with him and garner additional important information, and he saw in me an ally who would take sides with him against adversaries in the department who were antagonistic to him and music education.

Much to my astonishment and disappointment, I found out later that while he was encouraging me to move to Buffalo, he was seeking a position in the West. He was offered the position and accepted it; consequently, I was left to deal with adversaries of

IV: Pausing and Passing Midway (1972-1979)

music education on my own. It was not a pleasant experience, but I must say I matured in a hurry, perhaps sooner than I would have liked. Through it all, I managed to have the new programs I designed approved by the university undergraduate and graduate committees. I also established many associations outside the music department as well as a devoted following of students within and outside the department. The programs were widely accepted and acclaimed in spite of the offensive resistance I encountered from members within the department of music.

The success of the music education programs, as I should have anticipated, created envy and anger within the department. An acting chairman of the department, James Blackhurst, who was not a musician but a presidential assistant, was appointed during the time candidates for the permanent chairmanship were being interviewed. He was supportive of what I was doing and protected me and the music education program from the invidious attacks by an academic mafia, who, I believe, harbored unspoken anger possibly because many had never attained the appointments or prestigious positions for which they yearned. Moreover, many did not enjoy teaching and mirthlessly accepted it as an alternate to a famous career. One professor volunteered: "Pedagogy is an intrusion on my academic freedom."

Because some faculty had few students, and few were worthy, much time was spent jealously blocking the matriculation of and financial support for outstanding music education graduate students into the department. As a result, of the more than sixty doctoral dissertations and many masters theses I supervised over the span of my teaching career during my seven years at Buffalo, I was allowed to have only two doctoral students and one masters student. The students, one being Maria Runfola, were so good it was impossible to deny them admission, and only the masters student requested financial aid, which was minimal.

By the time the position of chairman was finally filled, the department was literally in shambles, particularly with regard to internal strife. Admittedly, the new chairman inherited a difficult situation, but his approach was such that the turmoil gradually grew worse. He was a music theorist and well aware of my criticism of how common practice music theory was being taught throughout the academic world. The chairman was teaching undergraduate theory himself, and in general the students were displeased with what they were learning and unhappy about what they weren't. They petitioned me to allow music students, regardless of their majors, to take music education courses to fulfill the first-year music theory requirement. My request to the music faculty to do this was granted. The courses, Tonal Imagery and Rhythm Imagery, would have been called Tonal Audiation and Rhythm Audiation had I coined the word "audiation" sooner. They were successful beyond my expectations and to such a degree members of the music theory faculty became uneasy about the comparison students were making between the two ongoing music theory curricula. Many students who were not majoring in music education requested permission to take the courses being offered by my colleagues and me in music education in lieu of the traditional offerings.

That was the beginning of the end. The chairman had a private meeting with me and stated that the music education faculty could no longer teach music theory, because students were not being prepared well enough to pursue sophomore music theory. When I asked for specific facts, none was given. Instead I was informed if I did not tell the students the current practice was to be discontinued, my academic life would become unpleasant. Mistakenly, I refused to cooperate. In time, my budget was cut and more irascibility was directed my way. I still refused to yield to the demands. As a consequence, the assailants organized and were able to divide the music education faculty into factions by promising special favors to anyone who would turn against me. The strong music education

IV: Pausing and Passing Midway (1972-1979)

program I had developed was virtually dismantled, and music education was reduced to the same state of mediocrity that existed before I arrived. As a result, the faculty was happy and comfortable once again. The only problem confronting them now was to find a new scapegoat to justify their incompetence. In time that became the chairman. Finding life in the department intolerable, I remained at Buffalo only another year or so. I knew I would have to leave sooner or later anyway because I felt isolated from the professional world. My work needed more visibility, and it seemed imperative that I secure a position in a university somewhere on the East or West Coast. When or where that would happen was not clear, but my departure was a certainty.

Of course, I associate some professional and personal satisfaction with my Buffalo experience. Professionally, with the invaluable assistance of Maria Runfola, I designed a unique five-year curriculum in music education, and it was immediately put into practice. The program became popular throughout the state and attracted many fine students. Those who completed all courses were awarded both bachelor and master degrees. Dan Belmondo, Clark Saunders, Art Levinowitz, and John Holahan were master's students from that program who followed me to Temple University where I oversaw their doctoral programs and was adviser for their dissertations. Also, I completed two extensive research studies. One was a five-year research study initiated in Iowa in which I compared the music achievement of privileged and underprivileged students. I found when given appropriate music instruction, students who attend inner-city schools achieve as well or significantly better, depending on their music aptitude levels, than students who attend suburban schools.

The second study bore on the difficulty and growth rates of the audiation of tonal patterns and rhythm patterns. Robert Moog and his associates, in their early Buffalo facility, designed and built unique computers and rhythm programmers for me to use to identify, perform, and record the thousands of patterns included in the study.

As an aside, I had ample time to analyze the data as a result of the Blizzard of 1977. It snowed continuously for ninety-nine days, and in time the university was forced to close. Fortunately I had collected all relevant output from the computing center the evening before the roof collapsed; it could not support the heavy snow. I remained at home for three weeks compiling information and shoveling snow from the roof of the house. There was so much snow surrounding the house, one could not see out the windows, and it would not have been prudent to try to open any outside doors.

One of the benefits accrued from lecturing and conducting seminars beyond my regular venue was the opportunity to meet many teachers and administrators. It was with their assistance I was able to secure an inordinate number of schools and students to participate in my various research studies. Kent Burchill of Niskayuna, New York, Shirley Friar of Cedar Falls, Iowa, and Arthur Schoenoff of Coon Rapids, Minnesota, were of great assistance in these endeavors.

On the personal side I had the good fortune to play bass in a faculty-wide jazz ensemble organized by Ira Cohen, a professor of psychology. Also, I found and bought a lovely house that needed restoration, for which I took much of the responsibility. It was commodious and fit my needs perfectly. My three girls came to visit during some of their school vacations, and during the summer months their stays were extensive. We had memorable times, and I believe their time spent with me helped alleviate some of the pain and hardship they were experiencing in Iowa City. On several occasions I thought they would remain with me permanently, but various concerns always prevented that from coming to pass.

About a year after I arrived in Buffalo, I met my wife to be, Carol Goodridge Beccue. We were married in 1976 and have remained

IV: Pausing and Passing Midway (1972-1979)

happily together ever since. Perhaps because this was a second marriage for both of us and we had learned to acknowledge what is important to develop a lasting relationship, we had the maturity and wisdom to appreciate each other and each other's needs. Carol was a longtime music teacher and choral director in public and private schools, and we tend to share many of the same values. We each take time to consider whether what one of us desires might actually be less important than what motivates the other. Over the years she has certainly become my best friend and confidant, not to mention the world's best unpaid private secretary, editor, and critic. The primary reason Carol married me, she says, was to help me find my soul and my waistline. I don't know whether she considers herself successful in those pursuits or whether she even still retains hope for the accomplishment of either.

In Buffalo I first experienced some national notoriety. I think as a result, Edward Harris, then president of GIA, wrote and asked me to visit him in Chicago to discuss the possibility of writing a book his company might publish. The meeting was fruitful, and we came to an agreement mutually attractive to both of us. I was eager to have a publisher who took a personal interest and who desired to print only material he believed worthy and respectable. Since then, all my subsequent work has been published by GIA. Ed and I have maintained an unprecedented author/publisher relationship pursuant to our first meeting almost forty years ago. Now his son, Alec, has become president of the company and continues to follow his father's philosophy as he directs a substantial part of the company's activities.

Special circumstances surrounded the need for my association with GIA. As I have explained, because I was unable to take my MAP royalties with me to Buffalo, I was bereft of research funds. Thus, along with the colleague whom I had brought to Buffalo and another former doctoral student who joined the faculty, Stanley Schleuter, we formed a corporation called Tometics. The purpose was to publish educational books and music anthologies supporting Music Learning Theory. The profits from the sales were to be used to establish a fund allowing the three of us to conduct research. I wrote the first book, *Learning Sequences and Patterns in Music*. It sold widely, and the profits were large. Our only costs were for the preparation and printing of the manuscript and for mailing and packaging because we were our own distributors. Unfortunately, while I was busy teaching, writing, engaging in research, traveling, and attending to departmental administrative responsibilities, one of the officers in the corporation, rather than writing scholarly books and doing research, chose to publish musical activities that bore a striking resemblance to musical crossword puzzles and other similar games. I was outraged. After many agonizing weeks of discussion and deliberation, it became clear my only recourse was to dissociate myself from Tometics by relinquishing all of my monetary interests for legal assurance my name would no longer or ever again be associated with Tometics. Obviously my association with GIA and the royalties I earned to support my research could not have come at a better time.

The music education profession began to take notice of my Prentice-Hall book, but much to my concern relatively little attention was given to my music aptitude test, MAP. School personnel were using it, but college and university professors either did not know it existed or pretended it didn't. Nonetheless, the three-year longitudinal predictive validity study of MAP was garnering high praise from psychologists and psychometricians, such as Robert Thorndike, in their books and reviews. Consistent with their usual response to my work, music educators gave it short shrift.

Those with praise referred to it as a paragon of scholarly research design that should be used as a model for validity studies pertaining to all types of aptitude tests. One influential psychologist, David Holland, went so far as to say had the study been associated with a discipline other than music, I and it would have instantly become world renowned.

A few faculty members at Buffalo were above the fray, and I enjoyed my relationship with them. We had mutual respect for one another, and I held their musicianship in high regard. Morton Feldman, a professor of composition, directed the June seminars in Buffalo. Through him and Lejaren Hiller, another professor of composition, I met and had opportunities for discussion with John Cage and other dignitaries who were frequent visitors to the campus. They broadened my musical understanding because I not only played bass in orchestras that premiered their works and that of other contemporary composers, but on many occasions we had lengthy discussions about music, music aptitudes, and the music learning process. On one occasion I was overwhelmed when Morton referred to me as the "Schenker of Rhythm." Whenever I felt depressed, Morty's wit and humor pulled me out of the doldrums. For example, when addressing a group he was asked what academic freedom meant, and he spontaneously answered, "The freedom to be academic."

Academic life for me at Buffalo and Iowa were poles apart. There was no Albert Hieronymus at Buffalo and certainly there was no Morton Feldman at Iowa; each had unique personalities and academic goals. Lukas Foss, who had been conductor of the Buffalo Philharmonic Orchestra until the year I assumed my duties at SUNY–Buffalo, remained friends with Carol after he left the city. She introduced me to him. Even though the time I spent with him when he visited Buffalo was limited, I was able to gain some unusual insights for research in music aptitude from him.

Claire Ives was a colleague of Carol's who taught English literature and composition in a junior college. Because Carol felt my academic writing was arcane, she casually asked Claire to look over one of my books and offer an opinion about my writing. Claire quickly agreed with Carol, and I concurred that I could use some help. She became my editor. This was the beginning of a long personal and professional friendship lasting until her untimely death.

My stay at Buffalo also resulted in a significant change in my personal philosophy. As one might imagine, I was born into a politically liberal family, a point of view I was expected to follow. Regardless of the candidate, the motto was always "Vote Democrat." I continued to maintain that view, though I must admit without much thought, until I encountered the faculty union at Buffalo. I disagreed with most everything they stood for, particularly strikes. Because of this, I was not held in high favor, especially by incompetent professors, some of whom served as union officers. At this time, my conservative leanings finally took root and have remained with me ever since. I had earlier inclinations to abandon my liberal stance when I was forced to contribute a portion of the salary earned for performing on recordings to the Musicians Performance Trust Fund established by the American Federation of Musicians. I had to join this national musicians' union to be allowed to engage in professional playing. James Petrillo was President of the union at that time, and it was his idea that those of us who were working as full time musicians should share our money and the glory of music with those who were less fortunate. Thus, daytime salespersons and others who dabbled in music but chose not to spend time and money for advanced music instruction were paid to perform at community events at the expense of those of us who were willing to give up many of life's comforts to advance ourselves professionally. That isn't even good socialism, as I understand it.

The negatives notwithstanding, all in all my experiences in Buffalo contributed clearly and significantly to my overall development. In addition to the few stimulating friendships I developed within the music department, several faculty members I met from other departments were also intellectually curious. In

IV: Pausing and Passing Midway (1972–1979)

Buffalo I was treated as a colleague, whereas at Iowa, no matter how well I fulfilled expectations, I was always considered by some as a student. I served on SUNY statewide search committees, including the one for the academic vice president, and I was invited to join a group primarily interested in semiotics. The weekly lectures introduced me to ideas that had never entered my mind and at the same time, they helped me collate thoughts that until that time were compelling but elusive. The summer seminars sponsored by the department of music education also provided for intellectual interaction among persons of diverse opinions, including some fine school music teachers. To be exposed to persons I believe respected me but did not always agree with what I was proposing was challenging and keenly invigorating. I grew immeasurably because we were all persistent in our points of view, but nevertheless open to change when confronted with commanding persuasion.

My benefits at SUNY–Buffalo were generous. Aside from all the typical advantages, I was entitled to avail myself of the assistance of a psychiatrist. Though I did not feel any great need for the service, being apart from my three children did take a toll. Moreover, I was curious about the psychiatric process. How better could I learn about it then by participating in it myself? The sessions took place before my remarriage and lasted almost two years, the amount of time I was allotted without charge. I concluded that I learned more about life in general than about myself. For example, a type of insanity was defined to me as "the combination of obsessions of very strong positive and negative attitudes directed toward the same object, goal, or idea." I found the freedom to say anything I pleased without fear of reprisal to be comforting, and I discovered that what tended to bother me seemed ludicrous when I heard myself talk about it. Whether the visits were responsible for actually changing me in a significant manner I don't know.

I was virtually isolated from academia during my last two years in Buffalo. I had resigned as director of music education, and my sole responsibility was to teach only two evening classes a week. Consequently, I was able to give attention to solidifying my ideas about rhythm in terms of macrobeats, microbeats, and rhythm patterns (rhythm patterns were initially referred to as melodic rhythm), and to develop the final version of rhythm solfege. Numbers were replaced with *du* to indicate all macrobeats in both usual and unusual meters, and microbeats in unusual meters were pronounced as *be* and *ba bi* rather than as *de* and *da di* in usual meters.

It was at this time I first became aware of the importance of body movement with deep breathing as readiness for learning rhythm. Most teachers are concerned with time (counting) and give little or no credence to space, the latter being best understood through movement. For example, a consistent tempo is not maintained simply by counting ongoing time. One must experience distance overtly in space between the punctuation of macrobeats before they can be audiated with covert accuracy in performance. So many teachers unwittingly emphasize dance steps that (for the most part) contravene free-flowing, continuous movement using large muscles of the body. Without exercising body weight in movement in place and space in initial rhythmic instruction, slow tempos tend to become slower and faster tempos faster. Given those research results, the effort motions of time, space, weight, and flow as explained by Rudolf Laban took on special meaning for me.

Also I was in the enviable position of having time to engage in research I had planned while I was still at Iowa but put aside because of other commitments. For example, I constantly wondered why music aptitude tests were suitable only for students nine years old and older. Other authors, as well as I, had come to that conclusion because the reliability of music aptitude tests used

IV: Pausing and Passing Midway (1972-1979)

with younger children was intolerably low. Was it simply a matter of the content and constructs of the tests, or was there something inherent in the minds of young children preventing them from responding to the tests?

During the development of the *Musical Aptitude Profile*, I had administered three of the seven subtests to children in kindergarten through grade three in order to gain additional insights into the validity of the battery. I found while kindergarten children who were identified by the supervisor of music in Ottumwa, Iowa, as having superior "musical talent" attained extremely high scores on one of the subtests (there were even two children who achieved perfect scores), the subtests were inappropriate for the majority of very young children. Following that, I directed the research of some graduate students in which they modified the recorded directions and added identifying colors to the answer sheets for the same three MAP subtests, then administered the subtests to second and third grade children. Ostensibly their results were the same as mine. We were obviously missing something or we were trying to change nature. I had to gain more insight into the problem.

With the luxury of time and the guidance of William Eller, a professor of education specializing in children's language development and literature, I began a self-instructional program by reading books on a child's comprehension of language and on the identification of words familiar to typical young children. I had surmised the problem with music aptitude tests for young children was not totally in the realm of music aptitude. The problem was somehow related to children not understanding the directions about what to listen for on the test recording and/or how to mark their responses on an answer sheet. Eventually, I designed an answer sheet that included pictures rather than numbers to coordinate what children were hearing with appropriate places on the answer sheet for them to mark their answers. Even more important, children were not asked to fill ovals on the answer sheets to indicate their answers; they simply had to draw a circle around a box containing two smiling faces if the two music patterns they heard sounded the same, or draw a circle around a box containing a smiling face and a sad face if the two music patterns they heard sounded different. Experimenting with the answer sheets apart from musical sound made it clear that children understood how to use the answer sheets in association with random sounds. Thus, I had solved one problem. The next problem to undertake, and the more important one, was to discover if the established psychological constructs of the measurement of music aptitude and thus, the intrinsic designs of music aptitude tests themselves, were different for younger and older students.

Based on some rather good hunches, I devoted myself to systematic empirical research of trial and error related to the content and construct validity of unique music aptitude tests of different designs. I then administered a variety of experimental tests to students of varying chronological ages in the public schools in the Buffalo area. I eventually discovered that to obtain satisfactory results, different types of music aptitude tests were necessary for students from ages five through eight, on one hand, and for students nine years of age and older, on the other. It soon became clear students were either in a developmental stage of music aptitude or a stabilized stage of music aptitude, depending largely on their chronological age. Thus, to obtain valid measures of their music aptitudes, either tests of developmental music aptitude or tests of stabilized music aptitude had to be administered.

One important distinction between the two types of tests is in a test of stabilized music aptitude, the recorded test questions must include both tonal and rhythm dimensions, but the student must be directed to attend to only one dimension or the other and to mark his or her answer accordingly. In a developmental music aptitude test, tonal and rhythm dimensions must be presented to the student in separate subtests. Psychologists such as Jean Piaget could certainly offer a strong explanation as to why that is the case, particularly as it impinges on the law of conservation.

There is little doubt other test developers were unable to construct reliable music aptitude tests for students below grade four because they insisted on using the same type of test for all students. In a stabilized test of music aptitude, musical context is important, that is, hearing a musical passage within the objective context of a given tonality and meter. In contrast, in a developmental test of music aptitude, the musical content is important, that is, hearing tonal patterns or rhythm patterns, not melodic patterns that combine tonal and rhythmic elements. In a developmental music aptitude test, tonality and meter are not established to assist children in comparing the content of individual tonal patterns and rhythmic patterns. Music aptitude level is determined by how well a child is able to subjectively intuit a tonality or meter that might be associated with a pattern heard apart from overall musical context. Although it is amply documented in several of my books and test manuals, one of the greatest nemeses I still face is trying to explain why a test of developmental music aptitude is not a music achievement test. For one thing, instruction relating to questions in a developmental music aptitude test does not take place formally in the classroom. The continued resistance that flies in the face of overwhelming evidence baffles and causes me distress. I hope someday I will learn to deal with the problem or simply ignore it. Through necessity I find myself moving closer and closer to the latter option day by day.

During my final years in Buffalo, I was involved in a spate of validity studies of developmental music aptitude tests, and I was also busy traveling and lecturing to acquaint persons with my research findings. By 1978, the *Primary Measures of Music Audiation* (PMMA), a developmental music aptitude test for kindergarten children and students in grades one through three, was completed and then published in 1979. That was accomplished as a result of the school administration with enthusiastic support of Ann Magavero of the board of education of West Irondequoit, New York, allowing me to administer and readminister the test over a period of one academic year to all students in kindergarten through grade three in the school district.

It soon came to my attention that students throughout the country who were exposed to high-quality music education programs were scoring relatively high on both the tonal and rhythm subtests in the battery, and thus, the results were not discriminating with precision among those students. The concept of developmental music aptitude became even more credible to me, and I immediately embarked on the construction of a parallel version of PMMA that embraced more complex music content. It culminated in the *Intermediate Measures of Music Audiation* (IMMA). I consider the identification of developmental music aptitude, in contrast to stabilized music aptitude, to be a major breakthrough in my work in the psychology of music. My mother would be pleased and my father astonished by this particular accomplishment.

IMMA was published in 1982, three years after I left Buffalo. Although it is designed for first through third grade students, much to my dismay it became common practice to administer it to students in fourth grade. Teachers preferred the two IMMA subtests, *Tonal* and *Rhythm*, to the two MAP tonal subtests, *Melody* and *Harmony*, because they required less administration time. Either the teachers did not understand or they did not care to know they were gaining expediency at the expense of some validity. However, as it turned out, IMMA was found to function reasonably well for fifth and sixth grade students, well enough that the publisher requested I provide norms and related statistical information for students in those grades. Because of this, an issue in my mind still remains a conundrum; whether developmental music aptitude resides in the mind or body, whether it is manifested in the content or construct validity of a test, or both. As I will relate, my later research addresses some of these relevant matters.

In addition to delving deeper into the nature, description, measurement, and evaluation of music aptitudes during my stay in Buffalo, I was concurrently engaged in research pertaining to Music Learning Theory. I remember during a lecture in 1974, I used the word "audiation" for the first time, and soon thereafter in 1975 I included it in an early version of *Learning Sequences in Music: Skill, Content, and Patterns*.

Good music educators have always taught with audiation in mind, but rarely (if ever) did they have a word to describe what they were doing. It was through necessity to explain the levels and sublevels of Music Learning Theory and how they interact that I was compelled to clarify the concept of audiation. Consequently, it has become part of Music Learning Theory. Moreover, the coining of the word provided the basis for my empirical research that describes the six stages and eight types that constitute audiation.

Little did I know at the time the impact the word would have on the music community at large. It has become a mainstay of the music educator's and professional musician's vocabulary in speech and writing. Some contrarians and the fainthearted still find it difficult to distinguish its meaning from inner hearing, imitation, memorization, and the like. How does one explain to persons what audiation is if they do not audiate? It is like trying to explain the difference between thinking and mindless memorization to those who do not have the mental capacity to think through what is being explained to them. Is it possible to explain the nature of intelligence to a person with limited intelligence?

The primary contribution of the idea of audiation is a musician may retain in memory and create and improvise music without the physical sound of music being present. Audiation requires that silent-sound in the mind be understood in terms of its intrinsic musical characteristics. Silence in music, as in speech, is essential for giving the listener time to make inferences about what has been heard, what is being heard, and what will be heard in terms of anticipation of familiar sounds and prediction of unfamiliar sounds. Audiation is to music what thought is to language.

At the height of my research output, officials at Temple University in Philadelphia contacted me and asked if I would be interested in teaching there. However, they also wanted me to become chairman of the department of music education. After my administrative experience in Buffalo, I had no desire to assume similar duties elsewhere. Among other things, I had learned that to have and retain power to improve a situation, one could not use it as one might choose. I declined the offer.

The following year they contacted me again and asked if I would consider a position as a tenured professor of music without administrative responsibilities. I visited Philadelphia and after a series of interviews, and with some reluctance, I accepted the position. Several of the faculty looked rather good on paper (a few had graduated from Ivy League institutions), but in-depth conversations proved to be rare, and more important, research and publication did not seem to be a priority. And for many, neither was teaching. Nonetheless, I was told I would receive full support in developing a PhD program in music education. At that time Temple offered only a Doctor of Musical Arts (DMA) degree, so I became somewhat enthusiastic about the opportunities the move would offer. Moreover, as I have already explained, I knew my work required more visibility, and midway between New York and Washington and in close proximity to Boston and Baltimore would be as good a place as any to satisfy that need. To be in Buffalo was to be hidden, and I had to rectify that situation as soon as possible if I were to more fully disseminate my research and make my publications more widely known. By this time in my life I was aware, although my accomplishments were due predominantly to hard work and perseverance, that I had developed a sense of self worth. Regardless of my limitations, I felt what I had to say needed to be heard because I believed it was important.

Carol and I sold our house, and in 1979 I assumed my duties in Philadelphia. We purchased a charming old commodious house on the main line in Merion Station, just outside the Philadelphia city limits. I was pleased when the earlier mentioned masters students from Buffalo with exceptional academic records chose to follow me to Temple and enter the doctoral program. Their presence contributed in large measure to the successful graduate program that emerged, one that attracted additional highly qualified students to the college of music.

V
The Philadelphia Story
(1979-1997)

The Temple University story is a long one, and it is difficult to decide where to begin. Upon my arrival in Philadelphia, I understood although I would not be chairman of the department, I would be director of the doctoral program in music education. Also, with the approval of the Seashore family, including sons, nephews, and grandsons, the Carl E. Seashore Chair for Research in Music Education was established for me. It always provided enough money to conduct my research. Additionally, a portion of research funds came from GIA, specifically a percentage of my yearly royalties, and other research monies came from registration fees collected for the annual summer seminars I taught at the Alfred Greenfield Sugarloaf Conference Center of Temple University in Chestnut Hill, Pennsylvania. Ann Casey, the outstanding director of the center, consulting with Carol and Roger Dean, chairman of the department of music education who organized the first seminar, made it possible for participants to enjoy the luxurious amenities offered by Sugarloaf at moderate cost. I will explain more about those ten-year continuous international conferences later in the book.

My teaching schedule allowed sufficient time to remain at home one or more days a week to do my writing or to travel for lectures and research activities. I was always free to accept lecture opportunities as I saw fit, and they became more numerous as the years passed. Nonetheless, my honeymoon with the college of music lasted only about three years, during which time I was able to design the PhD program in music education and win approval for it from the graduate college. By and large, the faculty and administration left me alone to do my work. I was attracting good students to the graduate program, and professors who taught in allied departments and colleges supported it. Perhaps that support was a product of my approach to graduate music education and its direct contrast to my predecessor, whose preoccupation was with aesthetic music education. Listening to, not performing music, was the prevailing emphasis at the time, and that approach was just another one of the eight- or ten-year cycling fads affirmed by the Music Educators National Conference (MENC). Fortunately, enthusiasm for this trend has diminished, and the idea has all but been abandoned by even some of its most ardent initiators. To champion listening without performance or performance without listening, either one without the other, is meaningless. Both performance and listening are fundamental to and necessary for the development of audiation.

With constant concern for my daughters and the experience at Buffalo still lingering, I was not in a mood to seek conflict with anyone. I simply wanted to do my work without disrupting the status quo in the department or college. I never commented on the music theory requirements or the way the subject was being taught, the complaints of my advisees notwithstanding. However, my desire for peace did not seem to be in the cards. I offered a graduate course in measurement and evaluation in music with emphasis on the construction of tests and rating scales. Students took the class as an elective. After assimilating technical information from my class about test reliability, one overly enthusiastic music education major asked her professor who was teaching a course in music therapy if it would be possible for her to peruse the corrected examination papers from a test administered the previous week. Her interest was more than altruistic; she received a low score. After she calculated the reliability of the test to be approximately .20, she announced her findings in a subsequent class and instructed the professor about the relevance of objective measurement to subjective evaluation, that is, to grading. The professor did not take kindly to this and soon appeared in my office with the chairman of the department of music education. I was informed from that point onward, no doctoral students in music education would be allowed to enroll in any music therapy courses. The professor's behavior was a rationalized response based on the erroneous assumption the student had acted under my direction and with my approval. There were no outward signs of the professor being uninformed might have been the root cause of the conflict.

Of course, this action created not only a personal problem for me, but a professional one as well, because when I designed the PhD program, I included two required courses in music therapy. Thus, I had to obtain approval from the graduate college to adapt the program, and though I managed that, it was no easy task. I was allowed to substitute six hours of electives outside the college of music for the deleted music therapy track. In actuality, the change turned out to be a blessing for the students because their formal and informal interests were broadened enormously. Needless to say, the music therapy professor became my unwanted enemy, and it did not take long for this adversary to gather cheerless compatriots among the faculty.

I'm certain the antagonist found assembling colleagues who already harbored some antipathy for me quite painless and gratifying. The faculty union at Temple was much stronger than the one at Buffalo, and despite great pressure and constant pestering, I refused to join. My students and I were even threatened during both faculty strikes when I crossed the picket line to teach my classes. The union asked I at least act duplicitously and cowardly, like some professors, and teach my classes at home if I really had to teach them at all. Of course, I felt the need to teach my classes. I was aware the majority of students who had come from distant locations to study with me had made huge sacrifices, often with families to support, and were living on borrowed money. To deny them instruction was total anathema to me.

I should also explain even merit raises were decided by the union. I was unhappy because in a departmental faculty meeting it was decided the procedure of rotating monetary raises among the faculty year by year, regardless of merit, would be continued. I strongly objected and said I would make the procedure public unless it was discontinued. My reaction dismayed others because at least one of them was not doing meritorious work, certainly not publishing. Moreover, there were constant complaints about the person's teaching effectiveness. Thereafter, raises were granted on the basis of scholarly achievement.

Some of my colleagues found fault with me on other issues as well. I was not paying homage to the DMA program in music education in place before I arrived. I viewed the DMA program as little more than a collection of several pick-and-choose non-challenging classes designed for those in need of graduate credits or seeking the title of doctor simply to increase their salaries and/or to retain or improve their teaching status. I think one faculty member was awarded the degree with only thirty credit hours beyond the master's degree. Though it was necessary for me to act as the advisor to students who had been pursuing a DMA under the professor I had replaced, few if any had not as yet identified a dissertation topic. I ultimately chose to disavow the DMA program and retain directorship of the PhD program. This

V: The Philadelphia Story (1979-1997)

decision convinced my colleagues that my students and I were elitists and believed ourselves to be superior to those in other programs. Considering the content and requirements for the DMA degree, it was obvious I had limited respect for the program. We all knew, even though we managed to exchange smiles when passing in the hall or at social gatherings, beneath our false sincerity we were not a particularly friendly or cohesive group, except when attacked from the outside. My outspokenness painfully highlighted the duplicitous environment and forced the faculty to avow this reality.

As the prominence of the PhD program grew (music education was the only department the graduate college that offered the PhD), about a dozen exceptional students living on and off campus were enrolled at a given time. I was advising all of them, and although usually no more than three or four were in the dissertation writing stage at the same time, I was able to accommodate most of their needs. However, my research and lecturing activities suffered as a result. Every one of the students eventually graduated, and they conducted respectable research to satisfy the rather rigorous dissertation requirements of the graduate college. I am proud many of those students have become prominent leaders in various facets of the music education world. Nevertheless, as I might have expected, there were disappointments.

First, a sizable number of my former students have become administrators and not productive researchers. However, as I look around the country, I find relatively few music education graduates continue to engage in research. Second, I keep in touch with only a few of my former students. A minority of them seems to have purposely created situations in which they have become adversaries, both personally and professionally. As I discuss this situation with other advisers who have directed a substantial number of doctoral dissertations, I find their experiences are not significantly different from my own. Perhaps there is something inherently wrong with doctoral curricula that engenders such behavior or there is a predilection on the part of some graduate students that foments those attitudes. Disappointments notwithstanding, I take comfort in having maintained splendid associations with select former students. With great satisfaction, I think of James Jordan, who has dedicated books to me and implemented much of my research in his writing and teaching; Cynthia Taggart, who has inundated school districts and early childhood music schools in Michigan with methodology incorporating Music Learning Theory and audiation; Janet Smith, who is teaching in Belgium and elegantly informing many Europeans about the value of Music Learning Theory and audiation applied to string performance; and Maria Runfola, who has sustained and maintains a vibrant music education program in Buffalo.

Typically, a graduate student majoring in music education takes entrance and exit examinations in music theory, music history, and music education. Rarely and not surprisingly, considering their self-serving needs, do theory and history faculty members find music education majors sufficiently knowledgeable in their disciplines. Amazingly, this is so even when some students have achieved superior grades in these academic courses as undergraduates in the same institution at which they are pursuing graduate study. Thus, in addition to the required music history and music theory courses, I advised students to enroll in supplementary classes to pass their exit examinations, referred to as written and oral comprehensives.

I have often wondered why administrators in music education have so meekly submitted to the rules initiated by music faculties that make the many hours required in music history and music theory courses mandatory for all students, particularly undergraduates, including music education and applied music majors. Perhaps without such requirements in place, music history and music theory classes would be bereft of students, as relatively few students are attracted to becoming music history or music theory majors. Even if more students were majoring in those disciplines, they would be capable of doing little upon graduation other than teaching music theory and music history to incoming neophytes, thus the infinite regression repeating the cycle with each new generation. It seems the purpose of teaching music theory is to teach others to teach music theory; I still find its impact upon genuine musicianship open to question.

Curiously, the accrediting agencies that eagerly support the idea that all music students should be required to take a series of music history and music theory courses do not support the reciprocal concept that all music students should elect at least one music education course. Regardless of major, the great majority of music graduates will at some time in their lives teach music, and often poorly, if their primary attention is given to the acquisition of instrumental and vocal techniques while all but ignoring the development of audiation and pedagogy skills. Be it good or bad, teachers find it easier and more comfortable to teach the way they were taught than to understand how students learn and how one ought to teach. Given that a professor cannot teach students how to teach but only give precision to their intuitive understanding of the teaching process, an introductory course explaining how students learn music would greatly benefit every student, particularly those who are studying instruments and singing. They are the ones responsible for the majority of private teaching that occurs throughout the world. Unfortunately, a common misconception is the better an instrumentalist or singer can perform, the better that person can teach. Nothing could be further from the truth. My experience is the correlation between the two pursuits is virtually zero, occasionally leaning to the negative side.

Contrast, if you will, the activities of a graduate student in music education with the curriculum of a student pursuing an advanced graduate degree in one of the sciences. Science students take only a few required generic courses and then quickly begin to work closely with a professor engaged in research of the student's chosen specialty. Obviously, these students have continual and sequential opportunities to grow and mature as they learn research techniques and become familiar with related scholarly literature. Perhaps that is why many are so successful as researchers throughout their professional careers. They learn what they came to school to learn, and they are not forced to spend the majority of their time coping politically, as they resentfully but quietly fulfill the wishes of those who have the power to make them do their bidding.

Most often, graduate students in music education enroll in courses that cover research during the first years of their attendance, which is far different from actual participation in research. One cannot foresee and write or lecture about the unique problems that forever present themselves as one is conducting worthwhile research. My students typically approached me to discuss a research topic at the beginning of their last year on campus (about two or three years after they arrived), or as they were about to leave to undertake a teaching position at another university (after satisfying all of their course requirements and passing the necessary examinations except for writing a dissertation). One can only imagine the frustration to be endured under those circumstances. Students seemed to be uninterested in designing research but not disinterested (unbiased) in the results of their proposed research. Far too often the situation required that I propose a research topic I believed to be of interest to a specific student, design the study, suggest analytical procedures, and oversee the writing of the document.

I was usually forced to assume the role of editor rather than of a reader who would be expected to offer helpful and insightful comments about the subject based on my experience. Students with English as a second language notwithstanding, I cannot help but believe much of the time devoted to music history and music theory would have been better spent in courses teaching students how to speak and then how to write the language. Not being a professional editor, I found attempting to be an editor the most distressing of my responsibilities in directing dissertations. Although denied openly by most engaged in higher education, the adviser of a student's scholarly work is as much on trial by the examining committee during and after the oral defense of the dissertation as is the student. Rarely do either students or professors understand that information without imagination is stagnant.

It is no wonder there is such a paucity of research in music education. I cannot help but sympathize with graduates who, as young professors, want nothing more to do with research. They experienced too much anxiety and humiliation in being expected to complete something they were unqualified to do and thus, associate those feelings with research. They have every reason to believe they are incapable of doing good research, and naturally, they desire to find something at which they can be successful. Often that something is administration. For, among other reasons, they have learned enough to know the underpinnings of the discipline of music education are shaky at best, and because of embarrassment, they choose to dissociate themselves from the profession. What seems to be most pernicious to me is they often advise whatever students they may have to replicate their own research because that is the only design and topic they even partially understand. Thus, in lieu of *bona fide* research, music education is inundated with a plethora of investigations from which conclusions cannot be drawn, and the circle goes round and round. Far too often, a turgid discussion section replaces a conclusions section in the written document.

When one of the music education faculty members at Temple resigned and went to another institution, the opportunity was created to hire a new colleague for the department who would be more in line with the philosophy of the program. Unfortunately, the practice common at many similar institutions at the time, which I believe continues to be so today, was to replace a full professor with an assistant professor. In that way, extra funds would be available to support favored undertakings. Given the low salary line, I had little choice but to choose one of my recently minted PhD students to fill the position. As I should have known, this did not work out well for a variety of reasons, and as a result, the program and I surrendered some credibility. In time, because the same financial restrictions applied, another person was given the vacant assistant professor position. Despite my requests, securing a full professor with an established reputation as a colleague who could share with me responsibility for teaching and advising highly qualified graduate students would not come to pass. That was the beginning of the demise of a rather spectacular PhD program, and to the satisfaction of a number of faculty members who felt daunted by the presence of an esteemed curriculum that attracted so many intellectually curious students with enviable reputations. Some of these students were beyond the professors' capabilities. Because the student grapevine was quite active, the students resisted and protested my suggestions that they enroll in some of my colleagues' courses offered primarily for DMA students. I deferred to the students' wishes, which further distanced me from the faculty.

The second person to fill the vacant position in the department was little improvement over the first. I identified the individual as a possible candidate after I was sent a teaching video in which the person used Music Learning Theory with a group of physically disabled students. While it was obvious some tenets of the theory were misunderstood, primarily because the person was ostensibly self-taught by reading my books, for the most part the teaching was impressive. As there were few other applicants with a PhD, the appointment was granted with the understanding, given a light teaching load, a considerable amount of time would be devoted to self-improvement. I think this individual's intentions were good, but for whatever reason or reasons, they were short lived. I suggested the person resign, and my suggestion led to a major confrontation. Allies, including the chair of the department, gathered and, primarily for personal reasons, took sides and persuaded the resolute assistant professor to join the union. It became evident to me I could never change the ambiance of the college. I won a few battles but, of course, I lost the war. I stood alone.

The person remained at Temple and, in time, was promoted and awarded tenure. I knew then after teaching more than fifteen years at Temple and being past my sixty-fifth birthday, it was time to retire from full time teaching. However, I did not submit my resignation until my last doctoral student completed the oral defense of her dissertation. I then accepted a position of distinguished professor in residence at the college of music of the University of South Carolina in Columbia.

As with my stay in Buffalo, there were extremely positive as well as negative experiences during my tenure in Philadelphia. My position at Temple certainly gave me the professional visibility I had hoped for, and because of special consideration given me by the administration in terms of time and money, I was able to take advantage of many opportunities. I lectured and offered seminars internationally. My first lectures abroad were in Germany in 1980, followed by England. Subsequently, I was, and continue to be invited to present lectures in Germany, Poland, Slovakia, Portugal, Spain, Italy, Korea, Austria, and Canada. In this country, in addition to the Sugarloaf seminars, I taught a special series of summer seminars at the University of Hartford in Connecticut, VanderCook College in Chicago, and Texas Christian University in Fort Worth. It was Ruth Whitlock, chairperson of music education at Texas Christian, who invited me to the school and introduced me to two commendable students, Alison Reynolds and Al Holcomb. During those years, I presented numerous lectures to faculties and students at other universities as well and to music teachers and administrators in public and private school systems throughout the United States. I also had the opportunity to meet Phyllis Weikart with whom I had many discussions involving the relationship of movement to rhythm, and Billy Taylor, with whom I exchanged thoughts about improvisation and music notation. Above all, I was afforded ample time to continue to engage in scholarly writing.

In addition, my work with early childhood music was featured on the *Today Show*, and I was interviewed more than once on National Public Radio on various topics. Several cassettes for MENC explaining the nature and use of music aptitude tests were recorded, and in 1994 "The Reimer/Gordon Debate on Music Learning – Complementary or Contradictory Views?" took place at the MENC national convention. Even with a busy schedule and without adequate collegiate support in the department, I was determined to assume my teaching and advising responsibilities with rectitude. For the most part, my students got along well, and they were always eager to assist one another in studying for examinations and other scholarly undertakings.

It was also during these years I was able to meet and develop a friendship with Donald Pond who was brought to the United States from England many years ago by Leopold Stokowski. Mr. Stokowski had sought Mr. Pond to teach at a prestigious private school in New York City. Donald later relocated to California where he collaborated with Gladys Moorhead in a special school established for the purpose of observing and documenting achievement in music as demonstrated in the daily activities of young children. We exchanged scholarly correspondence over a period of several years. It is my hope the similarities and differences in teaching and research highlighted in those letters will one day find their way into publication. The correspondence is part of the permanent collection of the Edwin E. Gordon Archive in the music library of the University of South Carolina.

While at Temple, the now celebrated annual one- and two-week Sugarloaf Seminars were initiated and conducted during summers. The lectures were devoted entirely to the theoretical explanation and practical application of Music Learning Theory and audiation and to novel approaches to understanding rhythm, music aptitudes, and relevant standardized tests and rating scales. Overall, the participants were nothing less than spectacular. Intellectually they were stimulating beyond my imagination and committed to raising the quality of music education in their schools and universities. Arthur Schoenoff, a former doctoral student at Iowa, brought a number of his music faculty from Minnesota public schools and others, such as Colette Wierson, Donivan Johnson, Leonard Upham, and members of the GIML board, attended often and from considerable distances to improve their musical skills and understanding of Music Learning Theory. Mary Ellen Pinzino, founder of the Come Children Sing Institute in Chicago, another Sugarloaf alumnae, continues to be one of Music Learning Theory's most ardent enthusiasts.

In 1987, I received the Christian R. and Mary F. Lindbach Award for Distinguished Teaching from Temple University, and largely due to the support of Bill Willett, who had postdoctoral studies with me at Iowa, I received the Third Master Teacher Award from the University of Hartford that same year. Perhaps my most prestigious honor was being selected as one of five Temple University professors to receive the Great Teacher Award in 1989. Attached to that award was a handsome sum of money I donated to the newly organized Gordon Institute of Music Learning (GIML).

In 1980 I had become acquainted with Richard Grunow, and we agreed to collaborate on the elementary instrumental music series *Jump Right In: The Instrumental Series*. This series put the Music Learning Theory I had been researching over a period of years into everyday practice. Later, Christopher Azzara and Michael Martin joined in that pursuit. Earlier, David Woods and I signed a contract with GIA to produce the classroom music basic series *Jump Right In: The Music Curriculum*, and it was to be coordinated with the instrumental series. Finally, I collaborated with Marilyn Lowe to create books and ancillary material for teaching piano based on the principles of Music Learning Theory. Needless to say, I was overjoyed with the prospect of my research findings being conveyed in such a manner that teachers could better understand the practical structure of Music Learning Theory and audiation.

Much to the credit and earnest efforts of Ellen Deacon, the first executive secretary of the Gordon Institute for Music Learning, this federally approved nonprofit organization was founded in the mid 1980s to disseminate the ever-growing base of research information on Music Learning Theory and audiation. Other early board members, music administrators, and university professors were Sam Ferrucci, Dick McCrystal, Mitch Haverly, Dick Grunow, Harry Semerjian, Alyn Heim, Robert Harper, Roger Dean, George Allen, and Maureen Carr. Their enthusiasm for Music Learning Theory had been largely generated through attendance at the Sugarloaf seminars. In addition to the national organization, several state chapters were organized as well as those in various European and Asian countries. Though GIML cannot boast thousands of members, that has never disturbed me. I am aware the immediate acceptance of new ideas is historically destined to a period of short duration.

I never desired a large audience for my work, only a thoughtful one comprised of intelligent musicians, and necessarily that excludes many who seek non-challenging professional support groups. Persons such as Dina Alexander, Michael Alvey, Terry

V: The Philadelphia Story (1979-1997)

Bacon, Jennifer Bailey, Eric Bluestine, Beth Bolton, Suzanne Burton, Richard Cangro, Pat Chiodo, Colleen Conway, Bruce Dalby, Denise Guilbault, Judy Heethuis, George Heller, Warren Henry, Ellen Hoard, Emily Jambeau, Heather Kirby, Diane Lange, Kathy Liperote, Gina Lee, Jennifer McDonel, Michael Mark, Herbert Marshall, Michael Martin, James Merrill, Jennifer Miceli, Debra Mitchell, Elaine Alba Mitchell, Michael Norman, Mary Louise Ott, Joohee Rho, Joanne Rutkowski, Peter Santucci, Christina Schneider, Erick Senkmajer, James Sherbon, Michael Slecta, Bruce Taggart, Lawrence Timm, Rick Townsend, Kenneth Trapp, Wendy Valerio, Krista Velez, Susan Waters, Marsha Whitman, and others have worked diligently in recent years to keep GIML vibrant and growing. I persist in my work not for outside approval, but for the self-satisfaction it provides me, as I am confident my research findings continue to grow stronger and stronger. Furthermore, I am delighted to have been characterized as "single-mindedly selfish and passionate about my work, an individual who will not be deterred from focusing on what is important."

In 1991, Volume II, Numbers 1 and 2, of the *Musical Quarterly* were devoted entirely to *The Work of Edwin Gordon*. The importance of my research and writings, however, has been recognized in various scholarly journal articles before and after that date. In all probability, such recognition contributed to my induction into the MENC Hall of Fame in 1996. Be that as it may, I cannot help but believe the pinnacle of my professional growth and development at Temple bears on my renewed interest and activity in early childhood music education and the composition of appropriate songs and chants for young children, which along with Music Learning Theory, audiation, rhythm, and music aptitudes has become a mainstay of my professional interest.

It seems clear throughout history all great advancements must be attributed to a small but persistent minority who had a sense of the difference between what is and what is not important. That is, they possessed an intuitive understanding of how the past and future blend into the present. This minority leads the way, and others who are less capable simply follow and ostensibly approve of what is happening. The few have always been patient, knowing full well change involves fear. Fortunately, I welcome change, because I believe growth cannot take place without positive change. Similarly, learning is not possible unless students are exposed to difference (such as improvisation) soon after they have understood sameness (such as imitation). Unfortunately, typical music instruction is a steadfast diet of imitation and memorization through listening to music and reading music notation.

I believe I have come to terms with the idea just as the most important things in music cannot be expressed in notation, not even vaguely, the most important thoughts cannot be expressed by either the spoken or written words. Nonetheless, reviewers of my work constantly criticize me for changing, as through I were unaware of what I was doing. When one is continuously engaged in worthwhile research, it is impossible not to change one's mind. I maintain everything I have written—books, tests, journal articles, and monographs—must be accepted as historical statements, which serve as guides, outlining what my thinking was in the past, and how and why it naturally evolved. I expect to keep learning and suggesting novel ways of comprehending the music learning process, thus continually modifying my beliefs to better achieve intended professional goals.

While at Temple, I devoted myself to thinking comprehensively about a variety of topics, all directly or indirectly bearing on Music Learning Theory. There was, of course, always Music Learning Theory itself. I taught, researched, and wrote, implicitly realizing I was only tapping the surface of understanding. I often wonder if all I have learned over the years will die with me because the limitations of language did not allow me to tell the whole story

V: The Philadelphia Story (1979-1997)

either when speaking or writing. Or might someone appear who could take up where I left off and continue the search for meaning? In other words, will there be another person with a similar variety of experiences that combine a unique type of musicianship, curiosity, motivation, integrity, and intelligence to truly understand and carry on this work? I don't expect a clone. However, I would be less concerned if I knew whatever I have contributed would not be in vain or run the risk of remaining unknown to others in the future. I don't use the word intelligence in a casual or flippant manner, as I have seriously thought about it for many years. I define intelligence rather simply: to have the stamina within oneself to be able to go beyond oneself, not to be dependent on borrowed ideas.

Perhaps if the premise that it takes a positive idea at least three generations to gain acceptance by the masses is true, my hope for music education, based on principles of Music Learning Theory, will come to pass in the lives of students of all ages sometime between 2025 and 2050, if in fact music education is still part of the school curriculum. It is possible I am taking time to write this history because I want to believe that after my death some persons will find these efforts valuable and will want and need to know more about the happenings underpinning my research and writing.

VI
Philosophy, Art, and Retirement
(1979-1997, continued)

I have come to accept the fact that even with the assistance of capable and practical editors and conscientious readers, most music educators still find my writings difficult to understand. I insist it is not the writing but the concepts many find difficult to comprehend. Oddly enough, educated individuals who are not professional musicians or music educators find my explanations understandable and interesting. Whether music educators do not take time to read and reread, or whether they are steeped in tradition to the extent they do not have the wherewithal to deal with the material, remains a mystery to me. Most of what I have to say has been said before by notable musicians and educators. The only difference is my writings have a research base, and I have arranged my ideas into a logical sequence particularly suitable for long-term practical application. Obviously, none of us has a corner on worthy ideas. Thus, it should be the responsibility of students and teachers to read available material and then create a viable approach to a personal educational process.

I expect readers of my work to understand what I have to say about learning and then comfortably merge it with their teaching personality and whatever method of teaching they favor. The fundamental issue for them should be how students learn, not how students should be taught. When teaching is the primary concern, the teacher's attention is directed to the class as a whole. However, when learning is the primary concern, the teacher's attention is directed by the individual student, and as a result individual differences among students become, as they should, paramount. With regard to judging students' progress, a capable teacher arrives at a bell-shaped distribution of grades when students are evaluated normatively (compared to one another), but all students receive the highest grade possible when they are evaluated idiographically (compared to oneself in terms of the relation of aptitude to achievement or present achievement to past achievement). Teaching is from the outside in, and learning is from the inside out.

After being at Temple for about five years, my intensive interest in early childhood music education resurfaced. This force resulted from two factors. First, I became suspect of the soundness of my own and others' research findings derived by using elementary school through university students as subjects. I became more convinced what I was finding with older students was due to their backgrounds, specifically what their exposure had been to music as newborn and young children. Thus, without accounting for variety in musical experiences, I believed the results of extant studies were not feasible and thus, could not be depended upon. It seemed necessary to reconstruct my research by working with very young children, and to carry out such research with any degree of credibility, I had to be involved personally with the actual teaching of children. With that in mind, I reactivated classes some graduate students had initially dabbled in at the Temple University Music Preparatory Department, located in Philadelphia. With the assistance of interested graduate students, I taught classes including young babies through children eighteen months old, children eighteen months to three years old, and children three to five years old over a period of years. Much to my

VI: Philosophy, Art, and Retirement (1979-1997, continued)

satisfaction, several of those who taught with me have become internationally known as successful leaders in early childhood music education.

The second factor compelling me to engage in early childhood music teaching and research is a bit more complicated. It had to do with my evolving negative attitude toward experimental research that, in my mind and those of reflective journal editors today, had been inevitably inseparable from the use of tests of statistical significance. As with the inadequate development of educational measures, when validity cannot be established for a test, the reliability of the test is spotlighted, and its low validity is intentionally buried and forgotten. What can be accomplished, rather than what should be or cannot be accomplished, becomes the focus of attention and, ultimately, researchers' and test developers' hubris.

There is a difference between statistical significance and practical significance, but the majority of professors of applied statistics and some theoretical statisticians teach only statistical significance. For example, at the conclusion of an experiment, when the mean scores of groups of students who received different types of instruction are compared to determine which type of instruction, if any, is superior to one or more, the probability of whether the difference between the mean scores did not occur by chance is unfortunately the first and usually the only issue. Fascination over whether the difference can be viewed with confidence, regardless of its size, sets the tone for interpretation. That is, hypothetically if the experiment were to be repeated a hundred times and if a difference as large or larger than the initial one was to occur a given number of times at a given level of confidence, it is reasoned the difference cannot be attributed to chance. The fact is, although it might be important to know whether a difference occurred by chance, in itself, that knowledge is not sufficient. What is more important and must also be known is whether that difference has practical importance. Given large enough groups of students, even a minute difference may prove to be statistically significant, but it may have no practical significance. Also, the dubious procedure employed to determine if there is a statistically significant difference between and among means should not be ignored. The calculations for proof simply and arrogantly bear on whether the variability in criterion scores between or among the groups is in fact greater than the combined variability in criterion scores within the groups and can be illustrated as such.

There lies the nub of the problem. Most researchers in music education are unaware of what constitutes a practical, important difference because their criterion measures are usually novel, unfamiliar to them, and, in most cases, invalid for their intended use. The criterion measures tend to be developed by inexperienced persons, often graduate students, to serve an immediate need. Further, when a published test with years of research data to support it is used as a criterion measure and thus suggests what an important difference might be, typically more enlightened persons discover the wrong test is being used for the wrong reason. Specifically, because of lack of a generally accepted music curriculum in most schools, cities, and states in the country, no base is available for administering a multilevel music achievement test that might be used to determine normal score increments per grade. Thus, without an understanding of what constitutes practical significance, most researchers are forced to be content with simply reporting statistical significance. Because of this situation, the results of much past research comparing the differences between and among mean scores through the use of tests of statistical significance is controversial at best, some of my own research notwithstanding.

Plainly, the issue is as follows: Does it make more sense to deal hypothetically with the probability of obtaining similar results if an

VI: Philosophy, Art, and Retirement (1979-1997, continued)

experiment were replicated 100 times, or to actually repeat the experiment one or more times with different students, teachers, and environmental conditions and determine if the results are similar on all occasions? I, of course, opt for the latter. Admittedly, the process is too long and arduous to expect of graduate students. Longitudinal research of that type should be undertaken by professors, but as I have mentioned, few of them engage in research, and those who do lack the ability of knowing what to do and how to do it. Also, the expense in time and money is, for the most part, lacking for the few who do have the qualifications to accomplish the work. Moreover, even when a statistical difference is uncovered, the most one should conclude is that there is sufficient evidence to suggest to other researchers it might be worthwhile to attempt to replicate the results. A final pronouncement based solely on statistical significance, typically made by inexperienced graduate students who complete only one investigation, is not warranted. Investigators bring unique backgrounds and experiences to research, and those factors interact with the results of the research and influence the interpretation of the findings. There may be only one truth, but it certainly takes on different forms and meanings.

I have only touched on one problem with experimental research in the social sciences. There are others. First, a prevalent assumption underlying the acceptable use of tests of statistical significance is, either knowingly or unknowingly, violated by researchers because of conditions beyond their control. When students in two classrooms participate in an experiment to compare the efficacy of two instructional methods, students from the two classes should be chosen at random to serve in one or the other group. This would necessitate changes in students' classroom assignments, and administrators are reluctant to make such changes. Moreover, a preferred teaching schedule cannot be followed because of conflicts with an established one. The consequences preclude the possibility of drawing valid conclusions based upon probability. Second, results based on tests of statistical significance may be generalized only to students, teachers, and schools that are highly similar to those that were studied in the experiment. Nonetheless, most, if not all researchers, ignore that fact and make sweeping non sequitur, resulting in misleading conclusions.

Another problem has to do with the difference between design and analysis in research. In the minds of most, the two are erroneously synonymous, or at the very least, confused. A common approach deals with analysis of data in an established manner with the analysis dictating the design. Actually, whereas analysis is a matter of tradition, the more important of the two, design, is a matter of creativity. Analysis looks backward, and design looks forward.

I trust you can understand why I became increasingly interested in doing thorough empirical research and observational investigations, especially in association with my early childhood music teaching. By carefully keeping records of musical behaviors of individual children, I began to collect evidence pertaining to normal musical growth. This evidence was vital to, among other important considerations, the validity of research I later designed in conjunction with older students. I determined what similarities and differences in musical ages emerged among groups of children of different chronological ages. Finally, I investigated the relation among musical behaviors I observed and music aptitudes, administering objective music aptitude tests to children as they got older and following their progress longitudinally from month to month or year to year, always searching for revealing relations between and among musical behaviors of children at various ages and music aptitudes.

Of course, I am compelled to deal with numbers to mark growth and determine similarities and differences among children. However, their use is not to be confused with the employment of

VI: Philosophy, Art, and Retirement (1979-1997, continued)

tests of statistical significance. I use numbers that give rise to averages only to investigate meaningful differences, and in time I determine the nature and value of those differences in terms of practical significance, not probability. What I have said, unfortunately for the wrong reasons, pleases many of those who lack the knowledge and skill to engage in empirical research and consequently champion qualitative research over quantitative research. The bane of my existence is attempting to explain to those persons that good research must combine qualitative and quantitative elements, both of which command respect. It is virtually impossible to accomplish creditable research without referring to the research of the past and without resorting to the use of numbers directly or indirectly, but not necessarily by employing tests of statistical significance. To prove worthwhile, the so-called qualitative element of research is based on preliminary research that offers some objective facts. Then the role of mature intuition is able to follow in a focused manner as the research enters further substantive stages. There is a difference between intuition and tuition (education). To engage in intuition bereft of a background in tuition always proves to be foolhardy.

Some words are in order about the bulk of my experimental research and investigations, much of which concerns the validity and other important issues relating to music aptitude and music achievement test batteries. I consistently use the statistical technique of correlation in all of its forms because the correlation coefficient represents an index that has been used over the years, and thus, it can be interpreted objectively. The point is because the index is patently objective, it renders the use of tests of statistical significance unnecessary. It is, itself, a measure of practical significance and in indirect ways, it suggests growth patterns.

As I look back on my last few years at Temple, I recognize many personal transformations, and not just in my attitude toward research. I became increasingly skeptical about the profession of music education. At the time, the role of music in the public school curriculum was not improving, and in my opinion it was becoming more tenuous. After more than forty years, I saw little improvement in the plight of the fine arts in the schools, and disillusionment was replacing my hope and motivation. The public was becoming less concerned with importance of the arts, and it appeared the primary goals of MENC were politics and advocacy, in the hope of attaining respect for school music. More and more music educators are now being chosen as chairpersons and deans of colleges of music. Perhaps it is because they are successful in being awarded outside funds and grants, or it simply might be when all else fails, why not see if music educators could save the day. I shudder to think how the hard-line academic music administrators of the past would have reacted to this.

It continually concerns me that I seem to stand almost alone, at least publicly, in my criticism of MENC leaders who routinely appear to grasp at straws rather than face the hard facts of how music is viewed by school administrators and parents. I believe such a professional organization should be making substantial efforts to support the development of viable music curricula and improve the musicianship of its teacher-members throughout the country. MENC and music merchants, who have instruments, music books, and related items to sell, appear to have joined together to invoke faulty publicity to convince the public of the value and importance of music education in the schools. Though many of their claims have proved untenable in the past, the bureaucrats in the national organization continue to foster them. Restating goals, changing their wrapping, and promoting them as new standards for school music accomplish little to improve teachers' music skills.

The ploy has become another mirage in the cycle of approaches MENC often promotes to cover up disturbing facts. I am thinking of one of the more recent trends supposedly relating to the important role of music in developing lateral dominance in the right hemisphere of the brain. Another example would be the emphasis put on politically correct multiculturalism to serve as a substitute for multicultural musicianship, of which most musicians, let alone music educators, are bereft. Standards mean little unless teachers, themselves, have attained them and understand how to guide students in achieving them.

The idea of enunciating expectations cannot help but become futile when the standards are idealistic, not realistic. Among other things, the standards are too general. They are impractical for older students who have not received the necessary preparatory instruction in the lower grades to meet successfully the higher levels of standards. Further, there is not enough time in the school day to address even some of the standards, and perhaps most important, many teachers themselves lack the musical skills to teach to the standards. How can anyone teach students to improvise if he or she cannot improvise? Furthermore, it should be clear to anyone with a modicum of insight into Music Learning Theory that improvisation cannot be taught any more than the act of thinking can be taught. The responsibility of music teachers is to provide students with the necessary readiness to learn (to teach themselves) how to improvise, and such readiness comes to the fore through teachers' understanding of curriculum development. Thus, to date, the cart has come before the horse. Just as the design of specific measurement techniques might give direction to lesson planning, curriculum might give direction to standards, not the other way around.

There are those outside the professional group of music educators, opportunists who for their own personal reasons and recognition side with bureaucrats and devote themselves to bringing the importance of music in the schools to the attention of the public. They have come as quite a surprise to the music profession at large because it is an uncommon happening. Rarely, if ever, did non-card-carrying music educators rally to such a cause. Nonetheless, they are doing the right thing for the wrong reasons, and sooner or later their attempts may boomerang and aggravate the real problems music educators are facing.

One ambitious philosophical psychologist promulgated the discovery of music being a separate intelligence among a dozen or so others that had to be nurtured. This discovery led many persons, among them the bulk of music educators, to believe the "revelation" came about through current research. They were even captivated by new intelligences continually added to the list. How was the average person to know that in 1904 in England Charles Spearman used the then-new techniques of factor analyses to conceptualize multiple intelligences? For all intents and purposes, the education community ignored the theory at that time. With its revival, music teachers and mandarins have gone wild with the idea, but they do not know what to do with it. It certainly does not afford them better ideas on how to teach; it only offers them propaganda to be used in attempting to persuade school administrators to publicly and privately acknowledge and give serious consideration to the efforts of music teachers. In my lectures, I have attempted to make music educators understand different types of intelligences should not be the compelling factor. The existence of multiple *musical intelligences* should be paramount, and teachers should make themselves aware of research explaining how to teach to the normative and idiographic differences of all students in an effort to meet individual musical needs. The implications for music curriculum development are enormous.

Also, there are psychologists who offered the startling finding that music instruction of young children enhances spatial intelligence, their research being supported in part by the music industry. What an effective boon for music educators! However, music educators did not take time to understand how the research was undertaken or the statistical procedures used to unveil the egregious conclusion. Upon replication of the testing a few minutes later, the supposed impact of music upon prowess in spatial intelligence actually dissipated. Notwithstanding the fact other researchers were unable to duplicate the results, it should be clear anything children are taught, not only music, is bound to increase their awareness; music is neither the rule nor the exception. Nonetheless, the sensational news traveled through various media sources, even prompting some state governors to offer CDs of classical music to parents of newborns. Suffice it to say, even if the report were true, should we then suppose music should be taught because it increases spatial intelligence? Does not the understanding of music have enough value in its own right to be taught for its own sake? Or, conversely, perhaps we should convince school administrators that spatial intelligence should become a staple of the school curriculum because it increases music achievement. It is obvious a threat to a profession will drive its constituents to any measure as long as it holds promise of enslaving the minds of those who need their thinking behaviorally modified.

My skepticism toward the profession of music education changed to cynicism when my research findings with young children were appropriated on many occasions without my specific knowledge to justify and support commercial early childhood music programs. I was able to complete my research primarily because I was not interested in money. Therefore, I did not need to cater to the whims of parents, who after a few years of note-reading piano lessons tend to generalize beyond their knowledge and tell music teachers what and how to teach. I was never paid for my teaching in the early childhood music program at Temple, though the graduate students were; the university retained all profits. Merchants of all stripes often capitalize on my ideas, and because of their limited exposure to and understanding of my work, they consciously or unconsciously misuse my findings, achieving sensationalism at the expense of vital guidance and instruction. Furthermore, I fear government bureaucrats in charge of school and teacher certification will begin to dictate what should be taught in early childhood music programs, how it should be taught, and who should be allowed to teach. Early childhood music education accreditation would then ultimately follow in the path of public school music dictates, largely fraught with personal and political implications and outcomes.

As I gradually became aware that my time at Temple and my career in routine university teaching were drawing to a close, my inner self was gesturing to me perhaps it would be best if I withdrew from all professional activities associated with my academic past. As I gave that possibility serious thought, it promised an immediate feeling of relief. On the other hand, it created anxiety and guilt. I had previously told Edward Harris, then president of GIA, I would join with four former doctoral students as coauthors to revise *Jump Right In: The Music Curriculum*. I could not resign from that commitment without causing my colleagues some consternation, not to mention the publisher, who had already invested money in the project. And I was in the process of coauthoring and revising books for *Jump Right In: The Instrumental Series*.

Also I must admit I became concerned about not having some intellectually curious students continually at my side, for without them I might quickly age beyond my years. I intuitively knew their perceptive insights motivated me and their supposedly naive questions always suggested relevant and far-reaching subjects to think about. I also had fleeting thoughts of revising the PhD program at Temple because after so many years I was able to explain to myself how it and the other similar programs I designed were misappropriated.

I came to understand an acceptable course of study leading to a doctorate in music education should provide students with an

VI: Philosophy, Art, and Retirement (1979-1997, continued)

early opportunity to engage in practical research. A reduction of courses in music and music education is mandatory, although an initial requirement of applied music seems necessary. And the reporting of research, both orally and in writing, and the interpretation of research needed to be emphasized. Most important, however, was something I knew I could never gain music faculty approval for, and thus, I gave up the whole idea. I would have liked to have approximately thirty of the sixty hour requirements beyond the master's degree be devoted to free electives outside the college or department of music in disciplines such as philosophy, literature, religion, drama, painting, sculpture, dance, movement, and so on taught by capable, caring, and sensitive professors. I know I personally acquired more important insights into the nature of audiation and Music Learning Theory from study in those disciplines than I typically took away from compounded study in music theory and music history. I believe students would profit from those types of experiences. If undergraduate instruction is adequate it would seem reasonable to assume the plethora of required graduate courses in music theory and music history is inordinate. Needless to say, I gradually found the process of having a committee oversee and approve a student's proposal for a doctoral dissertation groundless. I now believe one capable advisor should be solely responsible for that as well as for every other part of the student's research.

Thus, with a realistic look at my future and without undue deliberation, I took the bold step of disposing of my bass and bows, which I was using only infrequently, by taking them to New York City and putting them in the hands of a consignment merchant. He recognized the bass as one Philip Sklar had willed to me. You might think this would have been disturbing for me, but it was not. I am not certain why being parted from such an intimate part of my life went so smoothly, but I have a few ideas. As explained earlier, because my tonal aptitude is uncertain, I never considered myself to be or believed I could become either a first class classical or jazz bass player, but I did enjoy performing as an avocation. Nonetheless, although my sentiments were mostly with jazz, I was aware both jazz and jazz bass playing had passed me by long ago. Achieving the instrumental technique young bassists were currently demonstrating would have been in the realm of miracles. Certainly I enjoyed listening to them, intrigued more with *how* they were doing what they were doing than by what they were doing. However, I never had the desire to play like them. I was partial to my own style of playing, the prevailing mode during the 1940s. Unless jazz swings, it leaves me cold, and most of what I was hearing did not swing; it seemed more like a display of exhibitionist pyrotechnics.

Another reason I had little desire to perform was because there were so few musicians to perform with who played my style, and I was in no mood to play with the younger generation of pop musicians who indulge in endless repetitions of the same short melodic fragments. The musicians I once felt comfortable improvising with by performing variations of a pop tune chorus after chorus based on chord progressions and who often encouraged me to take solos, against my protests, were few in number. I never was a good soloist, my competence always leaning to the harmonic side. Whether I became weary of that type of improvisation because I had grown musically and wanted to hear challenging development sections (as personified by Paul Desmond and Gerry Mulligan) or because my musicianship was not at a level to understand how musical concepts had changed so rapidly, I do not know. Again, with regard to the younger set, I had no desire to participate in something that presented me with nothing but physical strain and boredom.

Before presenting my bass and bows for sale, I prepared for the event by involving myself in abstract, or non-objective, wood sculpturing. Unexpectedly, and perhaps even providentially, I had

VI: Philosophy, Art, and Retirement (1979-1997, continued)

been introduced to the husband of a friend of my wife, Bruce Johnson. Nancy and Bruce invited Carol and me to visit them in McLean, Virginia, where Bruce, a professional woodcarver, had recently added a very well equipped workshop to their home. Having always admired and enjoyed working with wood, I so appreciated Bruce's patience and the initial instruction he offered me in my early efforts. In time I converted a section of the basement of our house in Ambler, Pennsylvania, into a sculpting workshop. We had earlier moved from Merion Station because the area had become crowded. Sculpturing intrigued me and it became an elegant substitute for playing the bass for a number of reasons. Unlike other important parts of my life, woodcarving afforded the opportunity to slight reality and to indulge in imagination, which I could do alone and in silence. I captured space and expressed crystallized movement. What my art represents is far less important than what it expresses. That appeals to me greatly. However, it is not in the same league with my earlier unsophisticated interest in refinishing furniture. I particularly enjoyed working, intermittently placing my eyes afar as I carved, analyzing the process and investigating similarities to and differences from performing music. Specifically, I contrasted the improvisation processes in music and sculpture. In jazz bass playing I followed the chord progressions, and in sculpturing I followed the grain of the wood.

    I did not draw sketches of what I intended to carve. I began with a vague idea that soon changed into the shape for which the wood seemed best suited. In painting, the artist adds something, but in sculpturing, the artist takes material away. To me, the latter is certainly more provocative, because it brings to the fore the fact that less is more, and unlike in the painting process, what has been taken away cannot be replaced. The risk presents an awesome responsibility. Perhaps that concept alone is what sustained my interest in wood sculpturing as I had experimented to discover the ideal wood finishes that came to pass in my imagination. This pragmatic thrill would not have become restricted had my arm not begun to cause me excruciating pain as I would swing a mallet or sharpen a gouge and if my fingers had not become arthritic.

My happiness with wood has been a sharp contrast to my disillusionment with teaching that came about in my later years. It is difficult to know for certain why discouragement set in. Was it because I kept advancing in my knowledge and ability to teach and reality slipped by or because the backgrounds and experiences of students had been diminishing gradually over the years? Perhaps my ideas and thinking were advanced beyond students who did not have the readiness to comprehend what I was lecturing about. I felt alone in the classroom, thinking out loud. By the end of a lecture I became bored listening to myself. I would ask the majority of questions and proceed to answer them. The students who came alive could hardly find the words to ask a simple question that was muddling around in their thinking, and their primary concern was with the grade they might receive. It hurt deeply when I discovered I was more interested in a dissertation topic than the student pursuing it.

Even though students used language tolerably, they found themselves unable to communicate clearly. What they came to the university to learn seemed secondary, and many approached higher education as a shopping errand. In fact, one undergraduate student used that analogy to scold me in one of the last undergraduate classes I taught as a guest lecturer. He explained when going into a store, he found what he wanted on the shelf, paid for it, and then left. He came to class, actually thinking it only reasonable because he bought the course by paying tuition, I was to give him the product he purchased—my knowledge. For him to consult a book, the Web, the library, or even a dictionary in pursuit of supplementary knowledge was simply out of the question. He wanted to be told, not to learn. I sensed I was in the midst of a society without a culture. Perhaps I was, because I believe as soon as a culture begins

VI: Philosophy, Art, and Retirement (1979-1997, continued)

to lose its creative element, the culture is in a state of atrophy. I fear I see that frightful transition taking place in the profession from which I am in the gradual process of retiring.

In this same vein, I mention for one who has devoted so much of his professional career to educational test development, it is difficult to admit and to come to terms with the fact that many of the students who were taking my multiple choice and essay tests did not understand the test questions. I have no idea if they would have known the answer if they understood the question, and if they did, would the answer be too vague in their minds to actually express it? Further, there is always the gnawing question, even if students were capable of giving an ideal answer, would it relate to the validity of the purpose of the test? Classroom tests finally lost their appeal for me, but I was at a loss to know what to use as an appropriate substitute. Fortunately, I have never lost my zeal for refining and designing standardized tests of music aptitude and music achievement, as well as related rating scales and measures.

Although the writing of new books and the last revisions of my major books sustained my attention and distracted me from doting on the decline in quality of student adeptness and overall academic standards, I attempted to counteract my feelings of bewilderment by delving back into the research findings I gathered in the development of the *Instrument Timbre Preference Test* (ITPT). I was inclined to think perhaps the test was as sensitive to range as it was to timbre. By taking the two characteristics into consideration, I could revise the test and increase its validity. Also I was having a delightful time with persons making suggestions about how my books might be revised. Having been told my writing style is not reader friendly, I was prompted to write not only how I speak, but to write how students speak. Initially I found the latter suggestion intolerable and unacceptable, in fact, a horror. Soon they had their way. Computer-generated word lists convinced me of a sobering fact;

if I wanted college students of the mid 1990s to understand my writing, I had to pretend I was writing to typical twelve-year-old students of the 1960s. The point was made that contemporary students were having as much trouble reading my writing as I might experience with Chaucer's.

Another cause of my overall consternation with the academic world, music education in particular, was a result of Music Learning Theory seminars I was teaching in this country, in Europe, and in Asia. Aside from the fact that one-, two-, or three-week seminars do not provide sufficient time to allow teachers to assimilate new concepts and ideas I was presenting, the participants, many of whom were highly motivated veteran music teachers, lacked the audiation skills to understand and apply Music Learning Theory in their classrooms and studios. They were in pursuit of a panacea to solve problems they were encountering in the classroom, and they hoped Music Learning Theory and audiation would be the answers to their prayers. In short, though they could read notation and imitate and memorize music rather well, they could not audiate. They were proud they remembered from music theory classes that dorian, for example, "is from D to D on the white keys of the piano"; however, it had not occurred to them they could not audiate much beyond major and minor tonalities. They could talk about tonal solfege or rhythm solfege theoretically, but were limited in performing tonal patterns and rhythm patterns with syllables in even an elementary practical manner. Of course, facility with tonal syllables and rhythm syllables is fundamental to fully understanding and teaching the verbal association level of Music Learning Theory. Sadly, their sincerity in learning was overpowered by the restraints limited music achievement imposed. Audiation of tonal patterns in harmonic minor tonality, especially subdominant function, with or without solfege, was unapproachable.

I consistently encounter music teachers with far greater tonal ability than rhythm ability, and again, I discover that to be the case worldwide. They rush and slow tempos, find it difficult to discriminate among meters, and become lost when attempting to deal with unusual meters, those that are typically notated with the measure signatures 5/8 and 7/8. On various occasions I would model continuous flowing movement with all parts of my body and ask them to participate with me, but their rigidity was so encumbering they usually stood still and watched me in embarrassed amusement or amazement.

An additional problem is only a small percentage of teachers can improvise in any style of music. Without the aid of notation, the making of music is ostensibly an impossibility. What troubled me most was the realization that to teach Music Learning Theory, I had to defy the principles of Music Learning Theory. That is, for the sake of expediency, I was forced to teach the theory of music before the practice of music, and the symbols of music before the sound of music. I had to face the ridiculousness of needing to teach music theory to explain to music teachers how to begin to learn to audiate. This is tantamount to telling elementary classroom teachers they first need to teach students grammar so they can assist students in learning to listen to and speak a language. Perhaps now one can understand the disquiet I harbor with their college, university, and conservatory teachers, namely their music theory and applied music mentors, who are responsible for the unconscionable education students receive as they prepare to become professionals. I wonder if administrators in institutions of higher learning and bureaucrats in charge of the accrediting agencies have ever assessed their responsibilities. Are they truly unaware of the real world, or are they making do as painlessly as possible and waiting for retirement to come to pass?

Many observations influenced me as I deliberated my future. Just as soap operas seem to have more appeal than theater to the average person, I realized fragments of sound bites rather than music, as I know it, appeal to average persons, most of whom indulge in instant gratification. I felt disillusioned by the world around me. The music I valued was being ignored and forgotten, and what and who were referred to by the media as music and musicians were deplorable. Music educators were adhering to the only alternative that seemed plausible to them. Instead of teaching music, they were teaching about music, and they continued more aggressively to behave like metaphor merchants, traders in analogies, and symbol mongers. It seemed impossible to escape the thumping of car radios and the silent mouthing of words when waiting in traffic or to turn on the radio and hear popular music being rudely performed. My encounters with genuine country and bluegrass music were often a welcome relief, especially if the alternative was listening to the medicine men of sports doling out statistics to relieve the pain of reality to unknowing and unsuspecting masses for whom sports events become folk festivals. As technology in the production of music was gradually and tortuously speeding up and advancing beyond the public's ability to audiate, it became more and more believable that one's personal sensitivity and interpretation in the performance of music are indeed inseparable.

I retired from Temple at the end of December in 1996. Carol and I remained in our home in Ambler, both of us busying ourselves by fulfilling varying interests and traveling. Also, I continued to lecture overseas. When at home, I completed some rather respectable woodcarvings. Nonetheless, I became restless and began to seriously consider some offers that came forth from various universities to become associated with their schools on a part time basis. One of the schools Carol and I looked at was Iowa, my alma mater, but soon I realized I no longer belonged there. It's true; you can't go home again. The faculty had not materially changed, but I had. Nonetheless, visiting with my longtime personal friends in Iowa City made the thought of returning to my roots enticing.

VI: Philosophy, Art, and Retirement (1979-1997, continued)

The more we thought about retirement, the more attractive a move to the South became. Well we remembered our winters in Buffalo, and even Philadelphia snows seemed to require increased unexpected shoveling each year. We made several exploratory trips visiting Carol's brother in Florida and always stopping in Charlotte, North Carolina, to visit Dusty and Clay Pritchett, Carol's close friends from college days with whom she also worked summers on Cape Cod in the forties. As we passed through Columbia, South Carolina, we discovered what a lovely and charming historic southern city it is. Perhaps this would become the location that would fulfill the needs and satisfy the desires of our retirement years.

VII
More to Come
(1997-present)

No one from the University of South Carolina suggested I consider moving there until I presented a lecture in Columbia. A former student, who was chairman of the department of music and later was to become acting dean of the College of Music after its separation from the College of Liberal Arts, broached the subject. It took almost two years to work out the details with the permanent dean, Dorothy Payne, before I accepted the offer to teach there. We sold our house in Pennsylvania and bought a delightful condominium in the heart of downtown Columbia within walking distance of the university, the Statehouse and grounds, museums, and other city offerings. I enjoyed my office and partook in the privileges that went with my appointment, using the premises to store my wood sculptures until they could be properly placed in our living quarters. Upon my arrival in Columbia, I learned to use e-mail, and as I contemplate my addiction to it, I often wonder how I managed without it.

My position at the university was an interesting one. I had no special assignment, but I was invited to teach a course now and then and to guest lecture in some classes. I also was invited by the dean of the honors college to teach a course of my own choosing in that division. Additionally I consulted with graduate students as they pursued their research activities.

However, two things in particular pleased me. I was free to conduct research wherever and whenever I desired. Though I still found institutional committees that were organized to approve research proposals usually uninformed and annoying, I had the necessary financial support to study whatever piqued my interest. With credit initially to Jennifer Ottervik, and later with the facilitation and extraordinary cooperation of Dean Paul Willis and Louisa Campbell of the Thomas Cooper Library, space was made available in the music library to house the Edwin E. Gordon Archive. The collection is steadily growing, as is interest in the material that has been catalogued as well as displayed. The holdings are continually being organized for electronic transmission.

Shortly after our arrival in Columbia, I became intensively involved with a special research project at the University of South Carolina. It bears on harmonic improvisation. As explained, while in Buffalo I completed an eight-year study in which I developed a taxonomy of tonal patterns and rhythm patterns and investigated their difficulty levels and growth rates. In Columbia, I identified a hierarchy of harmonic patterns and subjected them to an analysis similar to that undertaken for the tonal patterns and rhythm patterns. As a partial result of my work, the *Harmonic Improvisation Readiness Record* (HIRR) and the *Rhythm Improvisation Readiness Record* (RIRR) were completed, both published by GIA. Aside from gathering crucial information about how students learn to improvise, pertaining in particular to the audiation of chord progressions and a sense of how temporal elements relate to giving harmonic changes contextual meaning, I believe I may have stumbled upon what may actually be generic forms of music aptitude. That possibility rises from the fact that the mean, the average score, on neither test increases in correspondence with the chronological ages of students in grades three through twelve. That consistent finding, which to my knowledge has not been uncovered for any other type of educational test, requires unique

VII: More to Come (1997-present)

interpretation, and further studies were and are continually being designed to serve that end.

One of my recent books, *A Music Learning Theory for Newborn and Young Children*, and two collections of *Songs and Chants without Words* have created more than a scintilla of criticism, primarily because of my novel ideas. However, most of what I know and pass on to others is based on empirical and observational research findings. For example, many traditionalists find it almost impossible to accept the fact that very young children can learn to audiate far beyond levels of many elementary school children and adults if they are guided appropriately in listening to songs and chants without words. Because of their familiarity with words, attention of children becomes misdirected, and, doing what is most comfortable and natural, they listen to the lyric of a song rather than to its resting tone, macrobeats, tonal patterns, rhythm patterns, tonality, and meter.

Also, when I engaged in early childhood music research, it was evident to me that to gain valid information about the music learning process, I had to observe the reactions of very young babies, many as young as a few weeks old and no older than a few months. Thus, I could study the learning sequence in its true form, one not interdicted by music achievement of any type. Colleagues and students thought the idea was not only radical, but outrageous, and that I would soon see the error of my thinking. In fact, many believed only children three years old and older have the wherewithal to be taught music, and they should be taught in the same manner as kindergarten children. It is not an exaggeration to say that had I not pursued my intuition, much of what is known today about music teaching and learning would have not come to the fore.

Nonetheless, despite animadversion directed toward my ideas and me by entrenched conventionalists, many of whom find it difficult to teach a song without words, I am amazed by the growing number of persons interested in my research and teaching. As a matter of fact, many of my ideas are creeping into the writings and publications of others as evidenced by the recent publication *The Development and Practical Application of Music Learning Theory*. More than thirty writers contributed to the volume.

However, the real issue is that young children should receive the best we can give them, regardless of who gets credit for breaking the code. Without recognition of the importance of informal and formal guidance that should take place in early childhood music programs to serve as a basis for success in more advanced music instruction at a later time, the future of overall music education is dubious.

Throughout my tenure at the University of South Carolina, the administration was experiencing disquieting changes. During the more than three years I was associated with the university, there were three chairpersons or deans of the college of music and two provosts. Many of the promises made would not or could not be kept, often one provost saying it was another who had made the commitments. I decided it would be best to really retire and spend my time with Carol, researching, writing, and lecturing, all of which contribute to my happiness and well being. Also, as a result of my sculpting being curtailed because of physical encumbrances, I developed a new art medium I call "squared abstractions" and "half-squared abstractions." The wall hangings, consisting of plaster, wire, string, and so on, have been referred to as "contemporary primitives." It was also during this time I directed Helena Rodrigues's PhD dissertation undertaken in Coimbra University in Portugal. I was pleased when she graduated with honors, and I was able to travel to Portugal to participate in the ceremony and festivities.

I submitted my resignation two years before my second contract ended, with the provision I be allowed to continue to assist a graduate student with the research she planned to undertake for her doctoral dissertation. An exceptional pianist, Ching Ching Yap, came to USC from Germany to work with me especially to learn about early childhood music and acquire skills associated with designing and conducting related research. My resignation was accepted with obligatory regrets.

Shortly thereafter, I decided it would be prudent for me to resign from the board of directors of the Gordon Institute for Music Learning. In my letter of resignation I asked to be placed on the honorary board. I had served more than ten years, two years as the founding president. It was my opinion younger persons with new and vigorous ideas would contribute more to the development of GIML than I could. Moreover, my interests were becoming so diverse, and the demands on my time more intense, I could not devote the necessary attention to the ongoing activities of the group. I keep in touch with board members and I have every reason to believe all is going well, although growth and increased membership is not taking place as quickly as they desire.

Following the Carolina experience, I was invited by James Forger to come to Michigan State University as a distinguished visiting professor and deliver lectures over a ten-day period. I accepted, primarily because of the work of a former student teaching there, Cynthia Taggart. Before I left the campus, I was asked if I would consider becoming a permanent professor of music at MSU. A plan was developed allowing me to remain living in Columbia and travel to Michigan twice a semester. Neither Carol nor I wanted to leave South Carolina, as we both continue to find Columbia a wonderful place to live. I would have no regularly scheduled classes to teach, but would be expected to consult with students and faculty, guide honor students in independent study, give guest lectures, and become heavily involved in research of my own choosing. I began my official association with the university in September 2001. Although my activities were stimulating, perhaps the most persuasive reason for joining MSU was the hope I would be able to reinstate a parallel of the Sugarloaf Seminars at Brook Lodge in Augusta, Michigan. Although the schedule created for me at MSU provided necessary time to continue lecturing in the United States and Europe, I found the driving regimen to East Lansing and back to Columbia to be burdensome, particularly in winter. The travel and the university's unanticipated financial restraints were the primary reasons I resigned, agreeing to fulfill only two years of the three-year agreement.

As birthdays pass, more and more my body reminds me of my age. Nonetheless, I continue to be ruled by my passion for research, and I am unable to give up my European lectures. The students and faculty are an inspiration, and I cherish the friends I have made. I teach in Poland every two or three years, where the *Polskie Towarzystwo Edwina E. Gordona* has been created and supported by the government. Ewa Zwolinka, Wojcech Jankowski, and Kasper Miklaszewski oversee the organization and the administration of the two-week seminars. In Germany, Wilfried Gruhn heads the *Gordon-Institut für frükindliches Musiklernen*; Almuth Süberkrüb organized the *Edwin E. Gordon Gesellschaft Deutschland e. V. Unabhäangiges Institut für Music Learning Theory, Musiklernen und Forschung*; and Maria Seeliger has arranged lectures in various cities throughout the country. In Portugal, Helena Rodrigues coordinates my teaching different years at Lisboa University and the Gulbenkian Foundation. Andrea Apostoli invites me to Italy once a year to teach for the *Assocciazione Italiana Gordon per L'Apprendimento Musicale* (AIGAM), the Italian counterpart of the Gordon Institute for Music Learning. Occasionally I give lectures in Seoul at the Gordon Institute for Music Learning in Korea. Also, I continue to teach and lecture on an irregular basis in other countries. In 2005 I traveled to Spain for the International Association of Registered Certified Tomatis Consultants, and in 2006 I will participate in

VII: More to Come (1997–present)

the International Orff-Schulwerk Symposium in Salzburg. In the United States, I teach two-week seminars every summer at Michigan State University and the State University of New York at Buffalo. On a more permanent basis, I have accepted the appointment of research professor at the University of South Carolina. It seems I am dissatisfied whether or not I am a part of a university. Nonetheless, my creative nature continues to find considerable fulfillment through improvisation generated by my art as it once was created through jazz and bass playing.

The more I lecture abroad, the more interest there is in having my books and tests translated into indigenous languages. This is true in Poland, Portugal, Italy, Germany, Japan, Korea, and China. Moreover, dissertations have and are being written in foreign countries as well as the United States about my research, my publications, and me. The subject of a doctoral dissertation at Temple University, completed in 2001, was a personal and professional biography.

My verve for writing and research has not diminished in the late seventh decade of my life, and, in fact, the twenty-first century may prove to be more productive for me than the twentieth. In the last few years, I have revised some of my earlier books and authored others. Some of my more recent books are *Introduction to Research and the Psychology of Music*; *Rhythm: Contrasting the Implications of Audiation and Notation*; *Preparatory Audiation, Audiation, and Music Learning Theory: A Handbook of a Comprehensive Music Learning Sequence*; *Rating Scales and Their Uses for Measuring and Evaluating Achievement in Music Performance Achievement*; *Improvisation in the Music Classroom*; *The Aural/Visual Experience of Music Literacy*; *Music Education Research*; and *Harmonic Improvisation for Adult Musicians*. GIA is now offering some of my older and popular books in a boxed collection with an accompanying CD. In addition to books and articles, I have recently completed the following research studies that are collectively published by GIA in monographs: *Studies in Harmonic and Rhythmic Improvisation*; *Test Validity and Curriculum Development: Three Longitudinal Studies in Music*; *Developmental and Stabilized Music Aptitudes: Further Evidence of the Dichotomy*; *Continuing Studies in Music Aptitude*; and *An Investigation of the Objective Validity of Music Audiation Games*. A new test is *Music Audiation Games*. A select list of my publications follows.

As I ponder the future, many pertinent and extraneous thoughts cross my mind. Depending upon one's place in life and what he or she may be thinking, one might discover some of those thoughts to be revealing, if not compelling. It is my hope that in time music educators will be able to diminish their insecurities and take a strong stand in making clear the possibilities music education has to offer. This lack of confidence may be observed in the attitudes of many recognized professional leaders toward one another. An example from my personal experience can be found in those individuals who have never published a valid test, yet conduct mindless investigations and write confusing and perfunctory articles purposely to reduce confidence in extant tests, but never take time to explore the possible useful qualities of the measures. Of course, doing so is a comparatively easy way to conjure a publication to support one's petition for promotion and tenure. I am told when insecurity becomes paramount, enormous energy is expended philosophizing about what is wrong with what colleagues have accomplished rather than in learning how to engage in complementary empirical research to further expand a specific body of knowledge. To attempt to improve one's academic position may not help the situation, but on the other hand, it probably would not make the problem worse.

I have spoken of Carl G. Jung, but feel the need to say a few more words about how his ideas have helped me satisfy, if not sustain, my lifelong curiosity about the absolute source and nature of music aptitudes. There is ample evidence that music aptitude is innate, not inherited. That is, although we are all born with a given level of music aptitude, what we are born with cannot be predicted from our ancestry, at least back through three generations. We owe what we are to the influence of all who have come before us, and what comes our way in terms of cognitive strengths and weaknesses (not necessarily physical traits) appears to be simply a matter of chance.

Moreover, music aptitude is not solely in the brain, but is also in the body. The body reacts through the senses and then sends significant messages to the brain to be stored. The brain might be thought of as the hard drive of a computer, whereas the body may simply reflect the software, without which the hard drive could not be activated. As in the continuous flowing movement of the entire body in the exploration of space, which is requisite for learning to maintain a consistent tempo in time, it is the body, not the brain (which I believe is highly overrated) that is fundamental to thought.

To attempt at this time to go beyond what I think I know about anything is tempting but precarious. The fulfillment and exploration of the future of knowledge would take someone who personifies Joseph Campbell's mythical hero and, unfortunately, I see no such person on the horizon. Perhaps the type of truth I seek can never be apprehended by those of us on earth. Such knowledge, like a conscionable description of Universal Energy or God, may be incomprehensible to the three-dimensional human mind.

As time passes and I keep protesting the possibility that my ideas may be superfluous, life becomes more mosaic with every passing day. My hope is I will have at least given as much as I have taken, and better yet, I will have given more than I have received. I am fascinated wondering who, if anyone, will finish writing all yet to be told and understood about the music learning/teaching process—discovering more about music from the inside out.

Publications

Articles

1961. "A Study to Determine the Effects of Practice and Training on Drake Musical Aptitude Test Scores." *Journal of Research in Music Education* 4: 63–68.

1967a. "A Comparison of the Performance of Culturally Disadvantaged Students With That of Culturally Heterogeneous Students on the Musical Aptitude Profile." *Psychology in the Schools* 15: 260–268.

1967b. "Implications of the Use of the Musical Aptitude Profile with College and University Freshman Music Students." *Journal of Research in Music Education* 15: 32–40.

1968a. "The Contribution of Each Musical Aptitude Profile Subtest to the Overall Validity of the Battery." *Council for Research in Music Education* 12: 32–36.

1968b. "A Study of the Efficacy of General Intelligence and Music Aptitude Tests in Predicting Achievement in Music." *Council for Research in Music Education* 13: 40–45.

1968c. "The Use of the Musical Aptitude Profile with Exceptional Children." *Journal of Music Therapy* 5: 37–40.

1969. "Intercorrelations among Musical Aptitude Profile and Seashore Measures of Music Talents Subtests." *Journal of Research in Music Education* 17: 263–271.

1970a. "Taking into Account Musical Aptitude Differences among Beginning Instrumental Music Students." *American Educational Research Journal* 7: 41–53.

1970b. "First-Year Results of a Five Year Longitudinal Study of the Musical Achievement of Culturally Disadvantaged Students." *Journal of Research in Music Education* 18: 195–213.

1970c. "Taking into Account Musical Aptitude Differences among Beginning Instrumental Students." *Experimental Research in the Psychology of Music: Studies in the Psychology of Music* VI: 45–64.

1971. "Second-Year Results of a Five Year Longitudinal Study of the Musical Achievement of Culturally Disadvantaged Students." *Experimental Research in the Psychology of Music: Studies in the Psychology of Music* VII: 131–143.

1972. "Third-Year Results of a Five Year Longitudinal Study of the Musical Achievement of Culturally Disadvantaged Students." *Experimental Research in the Psychology of Music: Studies in the Psychology of Music* VIII: 42–60.

1974a. "Fourth-Year Results of a Five Year Longitudinal Study of the Musical Achievement of Culturally Disadvantaged Students." *Sciences de l'Art Scientific Aesthetics* 9: 79–89.

1974b. "Toward the Development of a Taxonomy of Tonal Patterns and Rhythm Patterns: Evidence of Difficulty Level and Growth Rate." *Experimental Research in the Psychology of Music: Studies in the Psychology of Music* IX: 39–232.

1975. "Fifth-Year and Final Results of a Five Year Longitudinal Study of the Musical Achievement of Culturally Disadvantaged Students." *Experimental Research in the Psychology of Music: Studies in the Psychology of Music* X: 24–52.

1979. "Developmental Music Aptitude as Measured by the Primary Measures of Music Audiation." *Psychology of Music* 7: 42–49.

1980a. "The Assessment of Music Aptitudes of Very Young Children." *The Gifted Child Quarterly* 24: 107–111.

1980b. "Developmental Music Aptitudes among Inner-City Primary Grade Children." *Council for Research in Music Education* 63: 25–30.

1981a. "Music Learning and Learning Theory." *Documentary Report of the Ann Arbor Symposium: Music Educators National Conference*: 62–68.

1981b. "Wie Kinder Klange als Musik wahrnehmen – Eine Langschnittuntersuchung zur musikalischen Begabung." *Musikpadagogische Forshung* 2: 30–63.

1984. "A Longitudinal Predictive Validity Study of the Intermediate Measures of Music Audiation." *Council for Research in Music Education* 78 (1984): 1–23.

1985. "Research Studies in Audiation: I." *Council for Research in Music Education* 84: 34–50.

1986a. "A Factor Analysis of the Musical Aptitude Profile, the Primary Measures of Music Audiation, and the Intermediate Measures of Music Audiation." *Council for Research in Music Education* 87: 17–25.

1986b. "Final Results of a Two-Year Longitudinal Predictive Validity Study of the Instrument Timbre Preference Test and the Musical Aptitude Profile." *Council for Research in Music Education* 89: 8–17.

1986c. "The Importance of Being Able to Audiate 'Same' and 'Different' for Learning Music." *Music Education for the Handicapped Bulletin* 2: 3–27.

1988a. "Aptitude and Audiation: A Healthy Duet." *Medical Problems of Performing Artists* 3.1: 33–35.

1988b. "The Effects of Instruction Based Upon Music Learning Theory on Developmental Music Aptitudes." *Research in Music Education: International Society for Music Education* 2: 53–57.

1988c. "Music Aptitudes and Music Achievement." *Ala Breve* 35.3: 9, 10, 30.

1988d. "Musical Child Abuse." *The American Music Teacher* 37.5 (April/May): 14–16.

1989a. "Audiation, Imitation, and Notation: Musical Thought and Thought About Music." *The American Music Teacher* 38.3: 15, 16, 17, 59.

1989b. "Audiation, Music Learning Theory, Music Aptitude, and Creativity." Proceedings of the Suncoast Music Education Forum on Creativity, Tampa: 75–89.

1989c. Foreword. *Readings in Music Learning Theory*. Chicago: GIA.

1989d. "The Nature and Description of Developmental and Stabilized Music Aptitudes: Implications for Music Learning." *Music and Child Development*. Proceedings of the 1987 Denver Conference, St. Louis: MMB Music: 325–335.

1989e. "Tonal Syllables: A Comparison of Purposes and Systems." *Readings in Music Learning Theory*. Chicago: GIA: 66–71.

1990a. "Nowe testy badania zdolnosci muzycznych." The International Seminar of Researchers and Lectures in the Psychology of Music, Akademia Muzyczna im. Fryderyka Chopina, Warszawa, Poland: 300–310.

1990b. "Two New Tests of Music Aptitude: Advanced Measures of Music Audiation and Audie." *Measurement and Evaluation* 10: 1–4.

1991a. "Gordon on Gordon." *The Quarterly* 2.1–2: 6–9.

1991b. "Music Learning Theory in Preparatory Audiation." *Wahrnehmen, Lernen, and Verstehen*. Ed. Wilfried Gruhn. Regensburg, Germany: Gustav Bosse Verlag: 63–78.

1991c. "Sequencing Music Skills and Content." *The American Music Teacher* 41.2: 22, 23, 48–51.

1991d. "A Study of the Characteristics of the Instrument Timbre Preference Test." *Council for Research in Music Education* 110: 33–51.

1991e. "A Response to Volume II, Numbers 1 and 2 of The Quarterly." *The Quarterly* 2.4: 62–72.

1992–93. "Is It Only in Academics That Americans Are Lagging?" *The American Music Teacher* 37.5: 24, 25, 80–83.

1993. "Kodály and Gordon: Same and Different." *Kodály Envoy* 20.1: 22–28.

1994a. "Audiation, the Door to Musical Creativity." *Pastoral Music* 18.2: 39–41.

1994b. "Audiation: A Theoretical and Practical Explanation." *Kodály Envoy* 20.2: 12–14.

1995a. "Taking a Look at Music Learning Theory: An Introduction." *General Music Today* 8.2: 2–8.

1995b. "The Role of Music Aptitude in Early Childhood Music." *Early Childhood Connections* 1.1–2: 14–21.

1995c. "Testing Musical Aptitudes from Preschool through College." *Psychology of Music Today: Frederyk Chopin Academy of Music*: 170–176.

1996a. "Early Childhood Music Education: Life or Death? No, a Matter of Birth and Life." *Early Childhood Connections* 2.4: 7–13.

1996b. "Music Learning Theory." *Contemporary Music Education*. Ed. Michael Mark. New York: Schirmer Books: 169–180.

1997a. "Taking Another Look at the Established Procedure for Scoring the Advanced Measures of Music Audiation." *GIML Monograph Series* 2: 75–91.

1997b. "Music Education: The Forgotten Past, Troubled Present, and Unknown Future." *The GIML Audeates Special Edition*: 1–10.

1997c. "La Clase Colectiva de Instrumento." *Eufonia: Diaactica de la Musica*: 91–100.

1997d. "Early Childhood Music Education: Preparing Young Children to Improvise at a Later Time." *Early Childhood Connections* 3.4: 6–12.

1999a. "All About Audiation and Music Aptitudes." *Music Educators Journal* 86.2: 41–44.

1999b. "The Legacy of Carl E. Seashore." *Council for Research in Music Education* 140: 17.

2000a. "Contemplating Objective Research in Music Education." *Early Childhood Connections* 6.1: 30–36.

2000b. "Audiation: The Foundation for Music Improvisation." *Czlowiek–Muzyka–Psychologia: Akademia Muzyczna im Fryderyka Chopina*: 459–471.

2001a. "Contemplating Objective Research." *Audea* 7.1: 4–8.

2001b. "The Stakes Are Low But the Consequences Are High." *Council for Research in Music Education* 151: 1–10.

2003. "All About Audiation and Music Aptitudes." *The Grandmaster Series*. Music Educators National Conference: 13–16.

2004a. "Music Audiation Games: Comparing Youth and Adult Versions." *Audea* 10.1: 4–6.

2004b. "Pattern Preeminence in Learning Music." *Early Childhood Connections* 10.2: 7–17.

2005a. "Foreword." *The Development and Practical Application of Music Learning Theory*. Chicago: GIA.

2005b. "Vectors in My Research." *The Development and Practical Application of Music Learning Theory*. Chicago: GIA: 3–50.

Publications

Books

1971. *The Psychology of Music Teaching.* Englewood Cliffs, NJ: Prentice-Hall.

1976. *Learning Sequence and Patterns in Music.* Chicago: GIA.

1980. *Learning Sequences in Music: Skill, Content, and Patterns.* Chicago: GIA, 1980, 1984, 1988, 1993, 1997, 2000, 2003.

1984a. *Reference Handbook for Using Learning Sequence Activities. Jump Right In: The Music Curriculum.* Chicago: GIA, 1984, 2001.

1984b. *Study Guide to Learning Sequences in Music: Skill, Content, and Patterns. A Music Learning Theory.* Chicago: GIA, 1984, 1997.

1986. *Designing Objective Research in Music Education.* Chicago: GIA.

1987. *The Nature, Description, Measurement, and Evaluation of Music Aptitudes.* Chicago: GIA.

1990a. *Rhythm Register Books One and Two. Jump Right In: The Music Curriculum.* Chicago: GIA.

1990b. *Tonal Register Books One and Two. Jump Right In: The Music Curriculum.* Chicago: GIA.

1990c. *A Music Learning Theory for Newborn and Young Children.* Chicago: GIA, 1990, 1997, 2003.

1991. *Guiding Your Child's Musical Development.* Chicago: GIA.

1998. *Introduction to Research and the Psychology of Music.* Chicago: GIA.

2000. *Rhythm: Contrasting the Implications of Audiation and Notation.* Chicago: GIA.

2001. *Preparatory Audiation, Audiation, and Music Learning Theory: A Handbook of a Comprehensive Music Learning Sequence.* Chicago: GIA.

2002. *Rating Scales and Their Uses for Measuring and Evaluating Achievement in Music Performance.* Chicago: GIA.

2003. *Improvisation in the Music Classroom.* Chicago: GIA.

2004. *The Aural/Visual Experience of Music Literacy: Reading and Writing Music Notation.* Chicago: GIA.

2005a. *Music Education Research: Taking a Panoptic Measure of Reality.* Chicago: GIA.

2005b. *Harmonic Improvisation for Adult Musicians.* Chicago: GIA.

2006a. *Learning Sequences in Music: A Contemporary Music Learning Theory.* Chicago: GIA.

2006b. *Study Guide to Learning Sequences in Music: A Contemporary Music Learning Theory.* Chicago: GIA, 2006.

Monographs

1967a. *A Three-Year Longitudinal Predictive Validity Study of the Musical Aptitude Profile.* Iowa City: The University of Iowa Press.

1967b. *How Children Learn When They Learn Music.* Iowa City: University of Iowa, 1967, 1968.

1970. General Editor and Contributor. *Experimental Research in the Psychology of Music: Studies in the Psychology of Music.* VI. Iowa City: The University of Iowa Press.

1971. General Editor and Contributor. *Experimental Research in the Psychology of Music: Studies in the Psychology of Music.* VII. Iowa City: The University of Iowa Press.

1972. General Editor and Contributor. *Experimental Research in the Psychology of Music: Studies in the Psychology of Music.* VIII. Iowa City: The University of Iowa Press.

1974. General Editor and Contributor. *Experimental Research in the Psychology of Music: Studies in the Psychology of Music.* IX Iowa City: The University of Iowa Press.

1975. General Editor and Contributor. *Experimental Research in the Psychology of Music: Studies in the Psychology of Music.* X Iowa City: The University of Iowa Press.

1976. *Tonal and Rhythm Patterns: An Objective Analysis.* Albany: The State University of New York Press.

1978. *A Factor Analytic Description of Tonal and Rhythm Patterns and Evidence of Pattern Difficulty Level and Growth Rate.* Chicago: GIA.

1981. *The Manifestation of Developmental Music Aptitude in the Audiation of "Same" and "Different" as Sound in Music.* Chicago: GIA.

1989. *Predictive Validity Studies of IMMA and ITPT.* Chicago: GIA.

1990. *Predictive Validity Studies of AMMA.* Chicago: GIA.

1991. *The Advanced Measures of Music Audiation and the Instrument Timbre Preference Test: Three Research Studies.* Chicago: GIA.

1994. *A Comparison of Scores on the 1971 and 1993 Editions of the Iowa Tests of Music Literacy: Implications for Music Education and Selecting an Appropriate String Instrument for Study Using the Instrument Timbre Preference Test.* West Berne, New York: Gordon Institute for Music Learning Monograph Series.

2000. Studies in Harmonic and Rhythmic Improvisation Readiness: Four Research Studies. Chicago: GIA.

2001a. *Test Validity and Curriculum Development: Three Longitudinal Studies in Music.* Chicago: GIA.

2001b. *A Three-Year Longitudinal Predictive Validity Study of the Musical Aptitude Profile.* Chicago: GIA.

2001c. *Music Aptitude and Related Tests: An Introduction.* Chicago: GIA.

2002. *Developmental and Stabilized Music Aptitudes: Further Evidence of the Duality.* Chicago: GIA.

2004a. *An Investigation of the Objective Validity of Music Audiation Games.* Chicago: GIA.

2004b. *Continuing Studies in Music Aptitudes.* Chicago: GIA.

Tests and Manuals

1965. *Musical Aptitude Profile.* Boston: Houghton Mifflin.

1970. *Iowa Tests of Music Literacy.* Chicago: GIA, 1970, 1991.

1979. *Primary Measures of Music Audiation.* Chicago: GIA.

1982. *Intermediate Measures of Music Audiation.* Chicago: GIA.

1984. *Instrument Timbre Preference Test.* Chicago: GIA.

1989a. *Advanced Measures of Music Audiation.* Chicago: GIA.

1989b. *Audie.* Chicago: GIA.

1995. *Musical Aptitude Profile.* Chicago: GIA.

1998. *Harmonic Improvisation Readiness Record and Rhythm Improvisation Readiness Record.* Chicago: GIA.

2003. *Music Audiation Games.* Chicago: GIA.

Cassettes

1980. Lecture Cassettes for *Learning Sequences in Music: Skill, Content, and Patterns. A Music Learning Theory.* Chicago: GIA, 1980, 1984, 1988, 1993, 1997, 2000, 2003.

1981. *Tonal and Rhythm Pattern Audiation Cassettes.* Chicago: GIA.

1987. *Tonal and Rhythm Pattern Cassettes. Jump Right In: The Music Curriculum.* Chicago: GIA.

1989. "Testing Music Aptitude." *Voices of Experience*, 3019. Music Educators National Conference, Reston, Virginia.

1991. *Jump Right In to Listening.* Chicago: GIA.

1994a. "The Reimer/Gordon Debate on Music Learning – Complementary or Contradictory Views?" Music Educators National Conference. Reston, Virginia.

1994b. *Sid on Stage: A Glimpse of the Big Band Era.* Chicago: GIA.

2006. Lecture Cassettes for *Learning Sequences in Music. A Contemporary Music Learning Theory.* Chicago: GIA.

Music

2000. *More Songs and Chants Without Words.* Chicago: GIA.

Videos

1990. Video Guide for *Learning Sequence Activities.* Chicago: GIA.

1991. *The Importance of Early Childhood Music.* Hartford: Connecticut Public Broadcasting, Television Division.

1992. Video Guide to *Learning Sequence Activities: Jump Right In.* Chicago: GIA.

1999. *Music Play: Jump Right In.* Columbia: South Carolina ETV.